CH00967847

GRADUATE SCHOOL WITH HEIDEGGER

by

GREG JOHNSON

Counter-Currents Publishing Ltd.
San Francisco
2020

Copyright © 2020 by Greg Johnson
All rights reserved

Cover image:
Elihu Vedder, *The Questioner of the Sphinx*, 1863
Museum of Fine Arts Boston

Cover design by
Kevin I. Slaughter

Published in the United States by
COUNTER-CURRENTS PUBLISHING LTD.
P.O. Box 22638
San Francisco, CA 94122
USA
http://www.counter-currents.com/

Hardcover ISBN: 978-1-64264-125-7
Paperback ISBN: 978-1-64264-126-4
E-book ISBN: 978-1-64264-127-1

CONTENTS

FOREWORD

What a gift it is, to have this collection of Greg Johnson's essays on Heidegger available together in a real book, on real paper! All sorts of readers will appreciate Johnson's lively, unpretentious, and accessible presentations of Heidegger's thought, both those who have never read a word of Heidegger — and may thus stand in need of good reasons for doing so — and those, like me, who have been poring over the German philosopher's writings for years now.

Johnson gives due credit to the best academic commentators on Heidegger, such as Thomas Sheehan and Richard Polt. But there is one decisive respect in Johnson departs from mainstream scholars and proves to be a *far superior* guide to Heidegger's thought: his bold, open-minded, and honest treatment of all matters related to Heidegger's politics.

For Johnson, Heidegger is an "ethnic nationalist," which means that he believed that "the primary source of *meaning* in life and the primary source of moral and aesthetic *measure* is our *participation* in various ethnic communities — the very things that cosmopolitan, individualist, and technological man is concerned to have left behind" (p. 119).

Those who devote their careers to interpreting Heidegger's thought must believe that he has *something to teach them*, something that *differs from* and *challenges* the reigning ideas in academia and society at large. But this openness closes down when they encounter Heidegger's nationalist metapolitics and his radical critique of global liberalism. Discussions of Heidegger's politics are almost invariably prefaced by overt dismissal, repudiation, or self-righteous censure.

There are probably various motives behind these "politically correct rituals of execration" (as Johnson so aptly calls them): the need to appease leftist critics of Heidegger and protect one's reputation, perhaps also bad conscience for being intellectually drawn to reprobate philosophers.

Whatever the case may be, I suspect that behind all these

strategies for avoiding Heidegger's ideas about politics — be they *pro forma* or heartfelt — one will find an as yet unquestioned attachment to the modern understanding of man as an individual subject who believes that he can be *free* from what is simply given, or "thrown," to him — things like *ethnos*, tradition, homeland, and nature — and yet still live a meaningful life.

It is Heidegger who first and most radically brings this modern liberal concept of man into question. Those who are unwilling to follow him down this path thus demonstrate their unwillingness to entertain the possibility that Heidegger may be more or less *right* in his understanding of the most important things. And if one is not open to that possibility, can one even begin to understand him adequately?

Johnson, however, by virtue of his willingness to learn whatever he can from Heidegger's nationalist orientation, sheds light on many ideas that become hopelessly distorted and obscure in the hands of those who are unable to question their liberal assumptions about who or what they are as human beings (see, for example, Johnson's discussion, at once succinct and lucid, of "authenticity" and freedom on p. 124).

To conclude, Johnson's book leaves me with the hope that others will follow his lead and undertake a more serious, honest, and open-minded confrontation with Heidegger's thought — and the dangers that beset us, Western men, in the age of technological nihilism.

Anonymous Heidegger Scholar
Occupied Academia
August 17, 2020

PREFACE

I remember very clearly the first time I read Heidegger. It was a sentence from "What Is Metaphysics?" quoted by Ayn Rand: "Genuine utterances about the nothing must always remain unusual. It cannot be made common. It dissolves when it is placed in the cheap acid of mere logical acumen."[1] I found such writing repellent—but also somewhat fascinating.

A couple of years later, I had a bit of a chuckle at my own expense when I picked up Flannery O'Connor's short story, "Good Country People" and recognized myself in the philistine Mrs. Hopewell, who peeked in one of her daughter's philosophy books and found a similar line from "What Is Metaphysics?" about how science wishes to "know nothing about Nothing": "These words had been underlined with a blue pencil and worked on Mrs. Hopewell like some evil incantation in gibberish. She shut the book quickly and went out of the room as if she were having a chill."[2]

It's all too easy to complain about Heidegger's literary style. Heidegger is definitely one of philosophy's most difficult writers. But Heidegger wasn't incompetent. He was artfully and deliberately obscure. Such obscurity did not stop him from becoming the most influential philosopher of the last 100 years. In fact, it might have helped a bit. Heidegger was legendary as a charismatic lecturer. Some of that charisma lives on in his writings. Heidegger's style is part of his mystique.

Even though Heidegger didn't need popularizers to become famous and influential, he does need help to be understood. The essays, lectures, and reviews in this book are attempts to popularize Heidegger without vulgarizing him. Most were written for a non-academic audience of intelligent laymen. Two were

---

[1] Ayn Rand, *Introduction to Objectivist Epistemology,* expanded edition, ed. Harry Binswanger and Leonard Peikoff (New York: New American Library, 1990), p. 61.

[2] Flannery O'Connor, *Collected Works* (New York: Library of America, 1988), p. 269.

originally written as academic journal articles, although they were never published as such, and I have tried to remove all traces of pedantry. I have not, however, tried to remove all repetition. This is a collection of pieces written over a long period of time, not a unified treatise. Beyond that, some repetition is pedagogically helpful.

Most chapters fall into two sections, *Being & Beyond* and *Heidegger & Politics*, with the title essay in a class by itself. Each section begins with simpler essays and then gets more difficult. The fourth chapter, "Heidegger's Question Beyond Being," is the most "technical" and academic. If you feel bogged down, just skip to "Making Sense of Heidegger" and come back later. "Making Sense of Heidegger" is both challenging and long, but it is essential, so you need to persevere. The essays that follow it are a bit easier going.

The most important influence on my reading of Heidegger is Robert Sokolowski, who is best known as a Husserl scholar and an original phenomenological thinker. Sokolowski's classic *Husserlian Meditations*[3] begins by explaining three thought patterns that function as the grammar of Husserlian thought: the logic of parts and wholes, identity in presence and absence, and identity in manifolds. Once one grasps these thought patterns, reading Husserl becomes much easier, because even when wending through one of his labyrinthine sentences, one has a sense of where he is taking you.

Sokolowski's book *Presence and Absence*[4] is not specifically about Heidegger, but it nevertheless functions as a heuristic for reading Heidegger, who held that Being is an interplay of presence and absence, and whose primary criticism of both metaphysics and modern technology is their drive toward securing presence and abolishing absence. Once one reads *Presence and Absence*, reading Heidegger becomes much easier, because one can see where he is going.

---

[3] Robert Sokolowski, *Husserlian Meditations: How Words Present Things* (Evanston: Northwestern University Press, 1974).

[4] Robert Sokolowski, *Presence and Absence: A Philosophical Study of Language and Being* (Bloomington: Indiana University Press, 1978).

Another important influence on my reading of Heidegger is Thomas Sheehan. I discuss his work at length in chapter 5, "Making Sense of Heidegger."

Although I have a Ph.D. in philosophy, I am not a college professor or professional Heidegger scholar. So why am I, a mere amateur, publishing my thoughts on the Master from Messkirch? Because this is the kind of book that I wish I could have read when I was first struggling to understand Heidegger. It would have saved me time and trouble, steered me away from dead ends, and helped me pursue wisdom. Everything I have written is, in effect, addressed to my younger self and others in the same predicament. Heidegger has been a constant companion for more than three decades, a source of great pleasure and insight. I write simply to share those boons with you. I hope that someday Heidegger finds a popularizer with the literary talent and penetrating insight of Alan Watts. Until then, I hope this volume serves as something of a stopgap.

I want to thank the Anonymous Heidegger Scholar for his splendid Foreword, as well as Collin Cleary, Alex Graham, James O'Meara, Scott Weisswald, and Kevin Slaughter for helping bring this book to press.

I also wish to thank everyone who took my adult education class on "Heidegger, Metaphysics, and Nihilism" in Atlanta in the mid-1990s, as well as T. for the many stimulating hours we spent discussing Heidegger.

I dedicate this book to the memory of two Heidegger scholars: my teacher Thomas Prufer, whose seminar on *Being and Time* I am still catching up to, and my friend Charles Sherover, for countless hours of conversation on Heidegger, Kant, Leibniz, and Royce, as well as conservative politics and classical music. Something of them lives on in these pages.

Occupied America
August 17, 2020

HEIDEGGER WITHOUT BEING

The following brief introduction to Martin Heidegger's philosophy does not discuss the concept of Being (*Sein*), simply because there's no need to.

When understanding Heidegger, everything flows from the distinction between *acts of consciousness* and *objects of consciousness*. Acts of consciousness are *what we do to know things*. Objects of consciousness are *the things we know*. I see food and utensils on the kitchen counter, feel the knife in my hand, hear the sound of chopping, smell onions and rosemary, and taste the broth to see if it needs salt. I wonder when the guests will start arriving, glance at the clock to see the time, and ruefully recall the one with a history of lateness.

Every act of consciousness is directed toward an object of consciousness. This relationship is called *intentionality*, and specific acts of consciousness are called *intentions*. Intentionality does not mean "doing things on purpose," and in this context, intentions don't mean the motives or goals of action. Intentionality is the object-directedness of consciousness.

There are two basic kinds of intentions: *filled* and *empty*. An intention is filled when its object is present. When I turn for a knife, my intention is filled by the knife itself. By contrast, an empty intention is not filled by the presence of its object. Instead, it encounters the absence of its object. I open a drawer to find the vegetable peeler and discover its absence.

Our consciousness is a complex interplay of filled and empty intentions, of presence and absence.

But there's more to showing up than just being present. Even present objects are partially absent. When I look at the knife on the counter, the top side is present, and the underside is absent. But I see the *same* knife *in* its presence and absence. If I flip the knife over, the present side becomes absent, and the absent side becomes present. But the knife remains the *same*. Things show up through an interplay of presence and absence. We encounter them through an interplay of empty and filled intentions.

If the things in the world are never fully present, what about the self? There is nothing closer than our selves. Surely our selves are fully present.

Let's think this through. When I look at the knife, hear and smell butter sizzling in the pan, and rummage around for the vegetable peeler, these objects are present or absent. But I am not present. I am not focused on myself. I am focused on things *other* than myself. Moreover, if I were focused on myself, I would not be focused on the things around me. They would still be happening, of course. Smells and sounds and sights would still be bombarding me. But my *attention* would be focused inward, on myself. When I make myself present, the things around me become—relatively speaking, at least—absent, or I become absent-minded toward them. I could, of course, focus back outward at any time, and I might be jolted into doing so, for instance if the pan began smoking and the fire alarm went off.

To understand what is going on here, we need to make a distinction between *focal awareness* and *marginal awareness*. When we are focally aware of an object, we retain a marginal awareness of other objects. We can also switch our focus, making the margin the new center of our attention, while the former center becomes the new margin. Because we are simultaneously focally and marginally aware, the mind can be in many places at the same time. But the mind cannot be *focally* in two places at the same time. In order to focus on the world around us, we must not focus on ourselves. For the world to be present, the self must be absent.

But what if we set the world aside entirely and just focus on the self? Can the self be fully present to itself, fully transparent to itself?

Let's think this through. When we reflect on ourselves, we are taking the distinction between *acts of consciousness* and *objects of consciousness* "indoors," into the realm of consciousness itself. When I reflect on what happens when I find the vegetable peeler absent, I am turning an *act* of consciousness into an *object* of consciousness. But an act of consciousness can be objectified only by *another act of consciousness*. Consciousness can split itself in two, into an inner act and an inner object. And the inner act of consciousness can only do its job by being an act, which means that it will remain absent to us. We look *through* our acts of consciousness to their objects. When the act itself becomes present, the object becomes absent. Acts of consciousness can only do their jobs by not getting in the way — i.e., not becoming objects — by remaining as unobtrusive and undistracting as possible.

If reflection splits consciousness into an inner act and an inner object, then reflecting upon reflection itself requires a similar split. We have moved from cooking, to reflecting upon our awareness of cooking, to reflecting upon reflection itself. But reflection can be the object of a meta-reflection only if that act itself remains absent. This process can be repeated again and again — reflection upon reflection upon reflection, *ad infinitum* — but the distinction between act and object will always remain, and every act *qua* act will always remain absent. Thus consciousness can never be fully present to itself.

Consciousness is ultimately an activity, and as an activity, it can never be an object. When conscious acts are objectified, they are in effect dead. But a living act can never be an object. It is a blur, like the kingfisher in flight. You can try to grab the snake of consciousness, but it always slithers away, leaving its dead skin behind. Thus any attempt to speak about consciousness as merely an object is always inadequate.

Heidegger called the ultimate non-objectifiability of conscious life our "facticity." But doesn't talking about the non-objectifiable make it into an object? Yes and no. Yes, because everything we talk about is in some sense an object. No, because not everything we talk about is a well-defined, present object. Language can also point to absences and mysteries and blurs.

Heidegger invented the term "formal indication" for non-objectifying discourse about human beings. In *Being and Time*, he coins the term "existentials" to describe ways of speaking about human beings, reserving the Aristotelian "categories" to describe ways of speaking about things. From his earliest writings to the end of his career, Heidegger was focused on trying to find non-objectifying ways of talking about the human realm, which is one reason his work is so difficult to understand.

Thus far, our discussion of human consciousness has seemingly been entirely abstract and universalist, applicable to any man, anytime, anywhere. But that's not really true. I am writing this in English, my mother tongue. You are reading this in English, but for many of you, English is not your mother tongue. As soon as we learn to speak, our consciousness is bound up with language. Although the ability to speak is a universal trait of human nature, languages are not universal and natural. There are many different human languages, which vary from time to time and place to place.

If language is not natural, is it *conventional*, i.e., something devised as a medium of communication, like traffic signals, in which green stands for go and red stands for stop? Language isn't really conventional in this way, because to create conventions, we would need to *talk* about why we need them, what stands for what, how to implement them, etc. Which means that creating conventions *presupposes* the existence of a language. Therefore, language is not merely conventional.

Yet language cannot exist without mankind. We can, moreover, coin new terms and create conventions that become part of language. But for Heidegger, we cannot *ultimately* understand, create, or control language. Language is a practice that allows us to make things present. It is an activity of consciousness. Like all activities of consciousness, language can be reflected upon—but when it is active and alive, in the moment, it is absent. As an activity of consciousness, language is ultimately non-objectifiable.

Moreover, like all other meaningful social practices, we learn language by imitation before we are capable of self-consciousness and critical thinking. Languages and other social practices are traditions, passed down from time out of mind. Language may even be older than man, since we may have learned languages and other practices from our pre-human ancestors. Thus, at the core of the practices by which we make sense of the world, there is an unobjectifiable mystery that transcends each individual mind, merging us into myriad collective traditions that fade into the mists of unrecorded history.

Heidegger uses the word "humanism" for the idea that language and other meaningful human practices can be constructed and controlled by human consciousness. Heidegger is an anti-humanist, because he thinks it is closer to the truth that language, culture, and history construct the human mind rather than the human mind constructs language, culture, and history.

This is important, because from Ancient Greece to the present day, our civilization has been in the grip of diametrically opposed views of knowledge and power. When Plato denigrated sense experience and received opinion and claimed that true reality consists of unchanging "forms," or when Descartes discarded sense experience and tradition until he arrived at an unshakeable foundation ("I think, therefore I am"), *they were defining the real as that which satisfied their desire for certitude*, which was based ultimately in *a desire for power*. They were "humanists" because they defined reality as what satisfies human desires. This drive culminated in modern scientific and technological civilization, which defines the real as what is susceptible to scientific understanding and available for manipulation, control, and consumption.

Humanism is a profoundly self-alienating and self-destructive worldview, since it uproots us from the plurality of languages and cultures that give us meaning. It also abolishes all sense of limits to human knowledge and power—the whole dimension of absence, i.e., what escapes our knowledge and power. Humanism severs us from meaning and measure.

By destroying meaning, humanism condemns us to nihilism. By denying measure, humanism delivers us over to the unbounded pursuit of technological mastery over nature. I am going to call the complex of humanism, technology, and nihilism *modernity*, for short. The end result of modernity is the dehumanization of man and the devastation of the earth.

How, then, can we overcome modernity? Can we lay bare its roots, plan out an alternative, and then put that plan into action? Obviously, such a solution presupposes that we can understand and engineer human history—which is the very modernist delusion we seek to supplant. One can't fight humanism with more humanism. One can't fight modernity with more modernity. The solution to nihilism is not intensified nihilism. This is the lesson that Heidegger drew from his political involvement in the 1930s.

Heidegger's later philosophy is essentially a theory of historical change. As an anti-humanist, Heidegger does not think that human minds create history. Instead, history creates human minds. Modernity was not thought up by Plato, Descartes, and Nietzsche. Philosophers are not the hidden legislators of mankind. But they often offer the earliest and deepest articulations of fundamental changes in the *Zeitgeist*. To express the idea of historical change without an agent behind it, Heidegger uses the word "event" (*Ereignis*). The event refers specifically to fundamental transformations of *the meaning of everything*, such as the emergence of modernity — or its replacement with something else.

Modernists think they can understand and control history, but they can't even understand or control the emergence of modernity, which remains a mystery. Modernity wasn't thought up by modernists. Modernity wasn't imposed by modernists. Modernity is simply an event in the *Zeitgeist* that emerged from the inscrutable wellspring of meaning and has enthralled us.

But if modernity was not created and imposed by humans, then an alternative to modernity cannot emerge that way either. Anti-modernists need not despair, however, for if Heidegger is right about historical change, then our discontent with modernity is not merely subjective. We too are responding to a change in the *Zeitgeist*. There's nothing to prevent us from unplugging as much as we can from modernity, but we don't have to do the impossible to create a better world, for the change that we dream of is, in a sense, already real, and it is coming to meet us.

Counter-Currents, April 2, 2020

WHAT IS PHENOMENOLOGY?[*]

In *Being and Time* Heidegger transforms the central question of metaphysics—the so-called "ontological" question "What is Being?"—by applying Edmund Husserl's phenomenological method. So, to understand the project of *Being and Time*, we should answer two questions: "What is phenomenology?" and "What is ontology?"

HUSSERL & THE PHENOMENOLOGICAL MOVEMENT

The term "phenomenology" was first coined in eighteenth-century Germany. Johann Heinrich Lambert, a philosopher of the Wolffian school, used "phenomenology" in his 1764 work *Neues Organon* to refer to the theory of appearances. There is a section on phenomenology in Kant's *Metaphysical Foundations of Natural Science* (1786), and Hegel's *magnum opus* is the *Phenomenology of Spirit* (1807). But when someone refers to the "phenomenological movement" in philosophy, he is referring to the movement founded by Edmund Husserl.

Husserl was born in 1859 in Moravia, a part of the Austro-Hungarian Empire that is now part of the Czech Republic. Trained as a mathematician in Vienna, Husserl became interested in philosophy through the work of Franz Brentano—the same Franz Brentano whose book *On the Manifold Senses of Being in Aristotle* set Heidegger on his path to philosophy.

Husserl's first book, the *Philosophy of Arithmetic*, is an attempt to ground the concept of number in the counting activities of the human knower. Husserl's second book, *Logical Investigations*, was published in three massive volumes in 1900 and 1901. The *Logical Investigations* were immensely influential—on Heidegger and on German philosophy as a whole—and through them Husserl secured his first university appointment at Göttingen in 1901.

---

[*] Part one of the second lecture of an adult education class on "Heidegger, Metaphysics, & Nihilism" given in Atlanta in the mid-1990s.

Other Husserl works are the three-volume *Ideas* as well as *Formal and Transcendental Logic, Cartesian Meditations, The Phenomenology of the Consciousness of Internal Time,* and *The Crisis of European Sciences and Transcendental Phenomenology.*

In 1916, Husserl moved to the University of Freiburg, where Heidegger became his assistant. He retired in 1929 and lived a quiet life until his death in 1938 at the age of seventy-nine.

It was an outwardly uneventful life. Husserl was a kind and decent but uncharismatic man. Born a Jew, Husserl was a convert to Protestantism and a political conservative. Yet beneath his staid exterior was a vital and creative intellect focused with extraordinary intensity on what Husserl considered to be an infinite task of philosophical reflection.

Upon his death, Husserl left 45,000 pages of notes, comprising not only his lectures and book manuscripts, but also thousands upon thousands of pages of private philosophical reflections in which he constantly worked and reworked his ideas. These writings are probably the best documentation we have of the life of rigorous philosophical speculation carried out for decades with the highest sense of mission, simply as an end in itself. Husserl's writings are dense and difficult, rigorous and austere. His examples are drawn from the life of a scholar. His inkwell, for instance, is prominently featured in many of his writings as an object of intense reflection. Husserl was, in short, a consummate egghead. But this egghead launched a philosophical revolution.

THE PHENOMENOLOGICAL REVOLUTION

The guiding slogan of phenomenology is "To the things themselves." Husserl called this slogan "the principle of principles." For Husserl, the things themselves are not, however, the Kantian "thing in itself" that lies beyond the realm of experience. Husserl's principle means that the only authority for phenomenological philosophy is direct and immediate experience or intuition. Phenomenology takes what is given, simply as it is given, and tries to describe it carefully in its own terms.

Phenomenology is resolutely opposed to any form of reductionism. Reductionism is the view that one kind of thing is "nothing but" another kind of thing.

- ❖ Thales, the first Greek philosopher, declared that all is nothing but water—appearances to the contrary notwithstanding.
- ❖ Anaximenes declared that all is nothing but air—appearances to the contrary notwithstanding.
- ❖ Other reductionists declare that life is nothing but matter—appearances to the contrary notwithstanding.
- ❖ The individual is nothing but the sum of his social conditioning—appearances to the contrary notwithstanding.
- ❖ Religion is nothing but neurotic wishful thinking—appearances to the contrary notwithstanding.
- ❖ Mind is nothing but the brain—appearances to the contrary notwithstanding.
- ❖ Politics is nothing but economics—appearances to the contrary notwithstanding.

The reductionist method is to take two realms of experience—say matter and life—and declare that there is no ultimate difference between them. Life is "nothing but" matter, which means that the fact that living things *appear* to be different from inert matter is just an illusion; it is just "mere" appearance.

Phenomenology rejects on principle the attempt to claim that what appears to be different really isn't; it rejects the attempt to elevate some realms of experience to true reality and demote other realms to mere appearance. Phenomenology takes appearances seriously; it takes them at face value and simply describes how they are given. If living things appear to be different than inert matter, then that is good enough for phenomenology. The phenomenologist then tries to articulate the precise manner in which life appears to be different, and leaves it at that.

So, the phenomenological method is the attempt to carefully describe and catalog the different ways in which things appear. Phenomenology describes *how things show up* or *show themselves to us*. But, as stated, this is ambiguous. When we talk about how something appears, we can refer either to the *content* of its appearance or the *form* of its appearance.

If, for instance, we describe how a glass appears, we can describe its shape, its size, and its color. This is a description of the content of its appearance. Or, we can describe how a glass appears by noting the fact that it is a three-dimensional object, and because it is a three-dimensional object we always see only one side of it at a time.

A three-dimensional spatial object is not present all at once; all of its sides and aspects are not given at the same time. Rather, some sides and aspects — those that face us — are given to us directly, while the others sides and aspects, that face away from us, are not directly given; rather, we apprehend them as *absent* aspects that could be made present simply by turning the glass around to face us, thereby making the absent side present — but at the cost of making the present side absent.

This kind of description of how a glass shows up to us deals with the *form* of its appearance, not its particular *content*. The description abstracts out any consideration of the particular qualities of the glass and treats it simply as a three-dimensional object, then seeks to describe how it is given to us. And the description of the form of the appearance of the glass applies just as well to all other three-dimensional objects.

All three-dimensional objects have pretty much the same form of appearance, a form of appearance that differs from the forms of appearance of psychic states and of mathematical and cultural objects. Living things appear to us as having purposes and values, and their motions show up as actions in light of these concepts; dead material things appear differently.

Phenomenology leaves the description of the *contents* of the different realms of appearance to specialized sciences and sub-disciplines. The specialized sciences and disciplines divide the entire world up between them, and each sets busily to work describing and explaining the contents of its particular domain.

Because the entire world is divided up between these various disciplines, there would seem to be no phenomena left for phenomenology to study. However, because these specialized disciplines are so focused upon describing the contents of what appears in their specific domains, they overlook the forms of their appearance. The special sciences are so concerned with *what* appears that they give no thought to *how* it appears. They are so concerned with *looking at* what appears that they *look through* how it appears and thus *overlook* how it appears. Each specialized science has, therefore, a particular blind spot that is necessitated by the fact that one cannot be concerned with the form of appearances and the content of appearances at the same time. One's attention cannot be in two places at once.

Husserl's infinite phenomenological task was to describe and catalog all the different structures of appearance. To get a sense of how vast this project was and how picayune it could get, one of Husserl's students at Göttingen spent an entire semester working out a careful phenomenological description of a mailbox. Husserl's own work, however, was on considerably more important topics in logic, mathematics, the theory of knowledge, the philosophy of nature and values, and the philosophy of time.

PRESENCE & ABSENCE IN HUSSERL'S PHENOMENOLOGY

Although different kinds of beings have their appropriate ways of showing up, Husserl noticed a number of basic patterns shared by all forms of appearance. The most important of these patterns is what I shall call, following Robert Sokolowski, the interplay of presence and absence.[1] All objects of consciousness are given to us through an interplay of presence and absence. In Husserl's language, *empty intentions* refer to our awareness of absent objects, while *filled intentions* refer to our awareness of present objects. For Husserl, consciousness is always an interplay of empty and filled intentions.

It is natural to understand consciousness in terms of presence. But how does absence come into it? Your awareness of this

---

[1] See Robert Sokolowski, *Husserlian Meditations: How Words Present Things* (Evanston: Northwestern University Press, 1974) and *Presence & Absence: A Philosophical Study of Language & Being* (Bloomington: Indiana University Press, 1978).

lecture seems to be constituted out of various presences: our presence in the same room, the audible presence of my voice, and so forth. But presence is not what is essential to consciousness. Water may be present in a glass, but neither the glass nor the water is conscious of the other.

The wonder of consciousness is the ability to establish and maintain cognitive relationships with *absent* objects. If I pour water out of a glass, the relationship of presence between the two vanishes. But when this lecture is over, you can still talk about it, think about it, praise it, crack jokes about it, etc., even in its absence. The miracle of consciousness is our ability to talk behind one another's backs.

It is possible for us to be conscious of absent objects through the faculties of memory and imagination. We retain experiences in memory. In light of them, we can anticipate possible or even impossible experiences through imagination. Both of these powers are facilitated by, though not reducible to, language.

For Husserl, empty intentions have priority, in the sense that they are always there before they are fulfilled or not fulfilled by present objects. Thus cognition, for Husserl, always has an element of *re*-cognition, i.e., the experience of present objects as intended in their absence through language, memory, and imagination.

The claim that beings become present through presence and absence can, therefore, be understood as the claim that consciousness is most properly understood as an interplay between, on the one hand, the sensuous presence of the objects around us and, on the other hand, the faculties of memory, imagination, and speech that allow us to deal with beings in their absence.

How Phenomenology Might Save the World

At this point, one ought to be wondering just why phenomenology was viewed as such an earthshaking philosophical development. Hans-Georg Gadamer recounts an amusing story in his memoir *Philosophical Apprenticeships*:

I still recall how I heard the term [phenomenology] for the first time in 1919. It was in Richard Hamann's introductory art history seminar, where a kind of club came together for an exchange of views. Helmut von der Steinen led this memorable conversation in which the number of proposals for the renewal of the world was exactly equal to the number of participants. There was even a Marxist. . . . One person expected a renewal of Germany from Stefan George, another expected as much from Rabindranath Tagore, a third conjured up the giant figure of Max Weber, and a fourth recommended Otto von Gierke's theory of communal law. . . . Finally, someone declared with decisive conviction that the only thing that could save us was phenomenology. I accepted this devoutly and completely without even a shred of evidence to back it up.[2]

Phenomenology was remarkably popular for several reasons, all having to do with the fact that it stands as a corrective to the pervasive scientific reductionism of the time. Scientific reductionism has two dimensions.

First, there is the position known as scientific realism, which is the claim that the ordinary way people see the world is false and the way science sees the world is true. For instance, we experience a table as a solid object, whereas the physicist knows that the table is "really" nothing but a cloud of atoms and subatomic particles. It is more empty space than extended matter, and our perception of the table as solid is simply a naïve and mistaken theory.

We experience the table as colored, whereas from the physicist's perspective the table has no colors in itself and the color we perceive is a product of the interaction of our sense organs and the light reflected off the table—and the physicist's perspective is "true" and ours is "false." The table has no color in itself; it just has "reflectance properties" and our experience to the contrary is simply naïve.

Human beings experience space and time as elastic, depend-

---

[2] Hans-Georg Gadamer, *Philosophical Apprenticeships*, trans. Robert R. Sullivan (Cambridge: MIT Press, 1985), pp. 14–15.

ing upon their purposes and activities and their physical size and perspective. The trip home is always shorter than the trip away from home, even though one's watch and one's odometer register the same time and distance. The flight of stairs is longer at the end of the day than the beginning—but becomes quite short when one gets off work—even though the number of steps does not change. From a human point of view, buildings alter qualitatively as they grow in size, so that so many square feet of enclosed space alter when they are piled up together with ten thousand other identical units.

Scientific realism devaluates these kinds of experiences as mere illusions because they do not show up on objective scales of measurement. We should not feel any different if the same living space is on the ground floor of a house or small apartment building or on the top floor of a high-rise together with a thousand other identical units.

The result of scientific realism is the devaluation of the specifically human way of experiencing space and time, solids and spaces, colors and textures and their replacement with a so-called "objective" view of things that defines its objectivity precisely by the extent to which it abstracts away from the human way of experiencing the world. A world driven by scientific realism is a world in which human beings construct artifacts—and especially buildings and cities—that no longer bear any relation to the human way of experiencing the world. It is a world in which human beings feel dwarfed by and alienated from their own creations.

Husserl's phenomenology rejects scientific realism and treats the human way of experiencing the world as having its own dignity and integrity, which must be taken into account. In his last work, *The Crisis of European Sciences and Transcendental Phenomenology*, Husserl even argues that the world of lived human experience—which Husserl calls the "lifeworld"—has primacy over the world as it is modeled by science, and that science must ultimately tie its abstractions back to the lifeworld if they are to have meaning. A clear implication of this view is that technology must also tie itself back to the world of lived experience if it too is to be meaningful.

A second element of scientific reductionism is the reduction of human existence as such to non-human or sub-human phenomena. This kind of reductionism has many forms. Human behavior and experience have been reduced to the mere manifestations of hidden psychological, technological, economic, political, social, cultural, biological, and racial causes.

In each case, these forms of reductionism deny our experiences of such specifically human features as rationality, creativity, freedom, and responsibility—our ability to discover how the world works, to bring new things into the world, and to take responsibility for them. Phenomenology cuts this kind of reductionism off at the root, simply by delegitimzing the denial of the truth of our experiences of freedom and responsibility, rationality and creativity.

By undercutting scientific realism and reductionism, phenomenology undercuts some of the most militant and destructive ideologies of our time, such as Marxism and the cult of technological Titanism and unlimited progress—all of which depend upon forms of scientific reductionism and realism.

Another reason for phenomenology's importance is specifically philosophical. Reductionism is not just a staple of bad science and bad ideologies. It is also a feature of bad metaphysics. For instance:

- ❖ Many metaphysical systems argue that change is less real than permanence, or permanence less real than change.
- ❖ Some privilege sameness and deny the reality of difference.
- ❖ Others privilege difference and deny the reality of sameness.
- ❖ Some privilege mind and deny the existence of matter.
- ❖ Others privilege matter and deny the existence of mind.
- ❖ Some philosophers claim that intellect is primary and that sensations are but faint echoes of intellect.
- ❖ Others hold the exact reverse.

All of these positions use the same reductionist technique of taking one realm of experience, treating it as privileged, and treating all others as merely illusory projections or decayed versions of the privileged realm. So phenomenology has radical implications for the critique and refashioning of metaphysics.

This brings us to Heidegger.

Counter-Currents, March 4, 2015

WHAT IS METAPHYSICS?*

The best way of understanding what metaphysics is, is to understand what it is not. Metaphysics is not a specialized discipline; it is not a theoretical or practical inquiry that deals with a specific set of facts, or tries to change the world in a specific way. Every kind of fact and every kind of activity has some specialized discipline correlated to it. No matter what kind of facts you name, no matter how trivial, chances are that someone has written a doctoral dissertation on it—or will write one someday.

The specialized sciences and disciplines have divided up the entire world into separate domains of facts and parceled them out among one another. No matter what activity you care to name—from tying shoelaces to eating algae to rolfing to collecting mushrooms—there is probably some specialist in it who is willing to teach you how to do it, for a fee.

Metaphysics, then, cannot deal with facts, because all the facts are taken by specialized disciplines. Metaphysics cannot change the world, because all the activities that change the world are taken by specialized disciplines. So, if metaphysics does not deal with facts and does not change the world, what does it do? As Heidegger puts this question:

> The whole of beings is the field from which the positive sciences of nature, history, space always secure their domains of objects. Directed straight to beings, these sciences in their totality take charge of exploring everything that is. So it seems that there is no field of investigation left over for philosophy, although from antiquity it has been considered the fundamental science.[1]

---

* Part two of the second lecture of an adult education class on "Heidegger, Metaphysics, & Nihilism" given in Atlanta in the mid-1990s.

[1] Martin Heidegger, "The Idea of Phenomenology," trans. Thomas J. Sheehan, *Listening* 13 (1977), p. 111.

Metaphysics begins by taking a step back from action, from attempts to change the world. It is a reflective, contemplative activity that leaves everything as it is. Metaphysics also takes a step back from the specialized sciences and disciplines. And in taking this step back, metaphysics notices that each specialized discipline, because it is specialized, has two blind spots. These blind spots are, moreover, not merely accidental. Rather, they are essential to any specialized discipline as a specialized discipline. One's attention cannot be in two places at the same time. Therefore, in order for the specialized disciplines to catch sight of their specific objects, they have to be blind to other things. Specifically, the specialized disciplines are blind to two things: (1) they are blind to where and how their subject matter fits into the whole; and (2) they are blind to their own methodological and cognitive presuppositions.

First, because each specialized discipline focuses on its delimited subject matter, it overlooks the question of how its domain of facts is related to other domains of facts within the whole. For instance, biologists, insofar as they are biologists, deal with living things. However, when someone asks how life is related to matter, and if life can be reduced solely to material interactions, this is no longer a strictly biological question, for it cannot be answered with the tools and expertise of biology alone. It is a philosophical question, a question about how two domains of reality — matter and life — are related to one another within the whole.

In short, specialized disciplines deal with the *parts* of the world. Metaphysics deals with the *whole*. Metaphysics deals with how things — in the broadest possible sense of the term — "hang together" — in the broadest possible sense of that term (to borrow a phrase from Wilfred Sellars). Metaphysics deals with how all the different kinds of facts — all the different realms of being — are related to one another in the big picture. Thus metaphysics gives us a sort of map of the whole, showing how all of the parts are related to one another within it. And, because no map is useful unless it has a little "You are here" sign that allows one to orient oneself in relation to it, metaphysics is especially concerned with the place of man in the cosmos.

The second blind-spot of the specialized disciplines concerns how they know and go about studying their particular subject matters. Because each science is busy looking at facts, it *looks through* and therefore *overlooks* the cognitive faculties and methodological presuppositions that make its knowledge possible. For instance, many sciences use logic as a tool. They use it to look at the world, but they do not look at logic itself and ask about its nature and justification. This too is the task of metaphysics.

Metaphysics takes a step back from *what* shows up to us in the world and asks about *how* the world shows up to us. It does not deal with particular objects present to particular sciences. It deals with how objects are present to a human knower.

Metaphysics deals with the *presence* of objects, not *objects* that are present. Metaphysics seeks to detach presence from what is present. Metaphysics deals with presence as such, and tries to articulate its structure—for instance, in Aristotle's case, in terms of his table of categories and in terms of the principle of non-contradiction and the other laws of logic.

And, since presence is always presence *to* a knower, metaphysics deals with the human being insofar as he is a knower. So, again, human nature is a central topic of metaphysics.

The central question of metaphysics is the so-called "ontological" question, the question of "Being as Being," that Aristotle, in his *Metaphysics* (the first book to bear that name), describes as follows.

> The question that has always been asked and is still being asked today, the ever-puzzling question, is "What is Being (*ti to on*)?," that is, "What is Beingness (*ousia*)?" (1028b).

In Greek, the question of Being is "*ti to on.*" "*On*" is "Being." So the science of Being is "ontology." Ontology is the central branch of metaphysics. Aristotle arrives at the question of Being as Being by noting that the entire world of facts has been parceled out among specialized and partial disciplines.

As Aristotle puts it, the sciences deal with delimited realms and modes of being—fishy being and froggy being, physical

being and chemical being, social being and psychological being, etc. — but none of them deal simply with Being as such, ab-
stracted from all the different concrete ways of being.

The topic of ontology is Being as such — not being as fishy,
being as froggy — but simply Being as Being. It asks the question: "What is it to be — to be anything at all?"

It is Being that lies concealed in the blind spot of the sciences. It is ontology that disengages our attention from the objects
and practices that absorb the specialized disciplines and every-
day awareness. It is ontology that opens our eyes to their concealed background.

Ontology disengages our attention from the parts and turns
us toward the whole.

Ontology disengages our attention from the beings that are
present and turns us toward their presence as such.

Ontology disengages us from being absorbed in beings, and
turns us toward Being.

PHENOMENOLOGY & ONTOLOGY

Now, at this point, you should be wondering, "What's the
difference between phenomenology and ontology?" Phenomenology, after all, deals with how beings show up to us. It deals
with the presence/absence interplay through which beings become present. And ontology deals with the presence of beings
and its basic structures.

Phenomenology takes a step back from the partiality and
blindness of the specialized disciplines and asks how they and
their different domains fit into the whole, how the whole hangs
together. And ontology takes a step back from the partiality
and blindness of the specialized disciplines and asks how they
and their different domains fit together, how they fit into the
big picture.

Phenomenology gives man a central place within the whole,
for it is man to whom the world shows up. And ontology gives
man a central place within the whole, for of all the beings in the
world, only man asks the question of Being. It is man who notices the different kinds of beings in the world and thus divides
the whole up into parts. It is man who then wonders how the

parts fit together in the big picture. And if ontology deals with the presence of beings, then it must deal with man, for it is man to whom beings are present.

So, again: What's the difference between phenomenology and ontology?

This question is Heidegger's question as well. And his answer is: There is no difference between phenomenology and ontology, if we understand each of them properly. Heidegger claims, moreover, that phenomenology was implicit in ontology from the very beginning. He writes:

> Already in the beginnings something remarkable comes to light. Philosophy seeks to elucidate Being via reflection on the thinking of beings (Parmenides). Plato's disclosure of the Ideas takes its bearings from the soul's conversation (*logos*) with itself. The Aristotelian categories originate in view of reason's assertoric knowledge. Descartes explicitly founded first philosophy on the *res cogitans* [thinking substance]. Kant's transcendental problematic moves in the field of consciousness. Now, is this turning of the gaze away from beings and onto consciousness something accidental, or is it finally demanded by the specific character of what has been constantly sought for under the title "Being" as philosophy's field of problems?[2]

Heidegger's thesis is that the phenomenon that Plato and Aristotle called "Being" is the same phenomenon that later philosophers came to call "consciousness." It is the phenomenon that Heidegger calls "presencing" or the interplay of presence and absence, which is the topic of phenomenology. In the Introduction to *Being and Time* Heidegger states — first elliptically and then straightforwardly — the identity of Being and presencing, of ontology and phenomenology. He writes:

> What is it that phenomenology is to "let be seen"? What is it that is to be called "phenomenon" in a distinctive sense?

---

[2] Heidegger, "The Idea of Phenomenology," p. 111.

What is it that by its very essence becomes the necessary theme when we indicate something explicitly?

That is: What is the phenomenon studied by phenomenology?

Manifestly it is something that does not show itself at first and for the most part, something that is concealed, in contrast to what at first and for the most part does show itself.

That is: the phenomenon studied by phenomenology is not readily apparent; it is first and for the most part hidden or concealed. By contrast, the things that are readily apparent make up the world around us.

But at the same time it [this concealed something] is something that essentially belongs to what at first and for the most part shows itself, indeed in such a way that it constitutes it sense and ground [*Sinn und Grund*].

That is: The phenomenon studied by phenomenology may be hidden, but it is essentially connected with those things that are not hidden: the things that fill the world around us. The phenomenon that phenomenology studies is the "sense" and the "ground" of the things in the world around us. By "sense and ground," Heidegger means that the phenomenon studied by phenomenology is that which makes it possible for things in the world to show up to a human knower.

Heidegger then goes on to reveal that Being is the phenomenon studied by phenomenology:

But what remains concealed in an exceptional sense, or what falls back and is covered up again, or shows itself only in a distorted way, is not this or that being but rather, as we have shown in our foregoing observations, the Being of beings.[3]

---

[3] Martin Heidegger, Introduction to *Being and Time*, trans. Joan Stambaugh, in *Basic Writings*, ed. David Farrell Krell (San Francisco:

For Heidegger, the Being of beings is that which makes beings present to a knower.

Metaphorically, the Being of beings is the "light" in which beings show up to knowers.

Being is the process by which beings are disclosed or made manifest to us.

Being is the presencing of beings, the presence/absence interplay through which beings are given.

And, if Being is that which allows beings to show up to us, and if phenomenology is the study of the way in which beings show up to us, then *Being is the object of phenomenology.*

If phenomenology studies Being, and ontology studies Being, then phenomenology and ontology are simply two different words for the same thing: the study of Being.

Heidegger writes:

> Phenomenology is the way of accessing, and the manner of demonstratively determining, what is to become the theme of ontology. Ontology is possible only as phenomenology. The phenomenological concept of the phenomenon, as self-showing, means the Being of beings . . .[4]

Thus far, we have covered what phenomenology is and what metaphysics — or ontology — is. Phenomenology deals with the presencing of beings. Ontology deals with Being. We have also seen that Heidegger identifies Being with the presencing of beings through the interplay of presence and absence. He identifies phenomenology and ontology. Now is the time to make clear some of Heidegger's key terminology.

ONTOLOGICAL DIFFERENCE

Central to Heidegger's thought is the idea of the "ontological difference." The ontological difference is the difference between Being and beings. We are beings; the things in the world around us are beings. But Being itself is not just another being. It is not a being in the world. No matter where we go, we are

Harper, 1977), pp. 81–82.
    [4] *Basic Writings*, p. 82.

not going to find a particular being that is also Being itself.

Nor is Being a super-being outside the world. Being is not God, for God is a particular being.

Translated into the language of presence and absence, the ontological difference is the difference between presence and what is present, between absence and what is absent. The difference between a being and its presence and absence can be appreciated through the fact that the being remains the same, whether it is present or absent; thus it cannot be identified with either of the two.

Being is the presence/absence of that-which-is-present/absent. Presence/absence is always the presence/absence of that-which-is-present/absent, but it cannot be reduced to that-which-is-present/absent. Presence/absence is different from, but inextricably tied to, that-which-is-present/absent.[5]

THE METAPHYSICS OF PRESENCE

The central thesis of *Being and Time* is that throughout the history of ontology, the understanding of Being is determined by a particular understanding of time. Heidegger's task is

> . . . interpreting the very basis of ancient ontology in light of the problem of Temporality. Here it becomes evident that the ancient interpretation of the Being of beings is that it is oriented toward the "world" or "nature" in the broadest sense and that it indeed gains its understanding of Being from "time." The outward evidence of this—but of course only outward—is the determination of the meaning of Being as *parousia* or *ousia*, which means ontologically and temporally "presence." Beings are grasped in their Being as "presence"; that is to say, they are understood with respect to a definite mode of time, the present.[6]

---

[5] To adopt the maddeningly dense but clear and rigorous style of Thomas Prufer's "Husserl, Heidegger, Early and Late, and Aquinas" in his *Recapitulations: Essays in Philosophy* (Washington, D.C.: The Catholic University of America Press, 1993).

[6] *Basic Writings*, pp. 69–70.

This interpretation of Being in terms of presence is not confined to the ancients only. It is the underlying interpretation of Being throughout the entire ontological tradition. Jacques Derrida, following Heidegger, calls this interpretation of Being the metaphysics of presence. The "presence" in the metaphysics of presence has three dimensions. First, there is temporal presence, the present as opposed to the past and the future. Second, there is spatial presence, as opposed to absence. Third, there is cognitive presence, presence to a knower. The metaphysics of presence defines Being as that which is (spatially and cognitively) present to a knower in the (temporal) present.

The metaphysics of presence is an error, simply because it is a form of reductionism. Again, for Heidegger, Being is the presentation of beings to a knower through an interplay of presence *and* absence. Furthermore, Heidegger holds that this process is temporally dynamic. We make beings present in light of our projects for the future, which are based upon our pasts. The same world looks very different to us when we are running to and fro trying to meet a looming deadline or when we have no pressing engagements and a lot of time on our hands. So the way things show up in the present is determined by our expectations for the future, and our expectations for the future are determined in large part by what has happened in the past.

The metaphysics of presence seeks to eliminate this dynamic temporal dimension from Being, conceiving being as enduring, unchanging presence or substance. The metaphysics of presence also excludes the dimension of absence from Being. But this is an error, because time and absence are real aspects of Being, thus a good account of Being has to take them into account, not just leave them out.

DISMANTLING OR "DECONSTRUCTION"?

In section 6 of the second chapter of the Introduction to *Being and Time*, Heidegger claims that the metaphysics of presence is revealed by what he calls the *Destruktion* of the history of ontology. The translator renders *Destruktion* as "destructuring" but the more common rendition is "deconstruction," another term associated with Derrida. By "deconstruction" Heidegger means the task of taking metaphysics apart brick by brick and working his way down to the foundations of Western metaphysics in the lived experience of the Greek philosophers.

Deconstruction does not mean destruction. It is not an attempt to raze metaphysics to the ground and start over. Rather, it is the attempt to recover the original motivating experiences that got metaphysics going in the first place. Specifically, it tries to recover the temporal dynamism and absential aspects of Being and tries to figure out why they were later passed over.

DASEIN

The word "*Dasein*" appears frequently in Heidegger translations. It is capitalized and usually is not in italics. Years ago, a friend told me the story of a woman who started reading Heidegger but quickly stopped because she concluded that she would first have to read this Dasein person Heidegger kept mentioning. So, who is this Dasein person? The answer is: You are Dasein. *Dasein* is not a proper name. *Dasein* is the knower to whom beings are present.

But why does Heidegger use the word "*Dasein*"? why not simply use the word "knower" or "subject" or "human being"? *Dasein* is a German word for existence, for concrete thereness. Heidegger, however, hears *Dasein* as a compound of two other German words: *Da* and *Sein*. *Da* means both here and there. It means the place or the whereabouts of something. *Sein* is the German word that we translate as "Being" with a big "B."

Putting the two together, Heidegger uses the word *Dasein* to mean the place of Being or the whereabouts of Being. *Dasein*, as the one to whom beings show up, is the place of this showing. This showing is Being. So *Dasein* is the place of Being.

Heidegger speaks of *Dasein* rather than "human being," "reason," or "subjectivity" because he wants to resist the universalism implicit in these concepts. Human nature is one and the same; reason is one and the same; subjectivity is one and the same. Which would imply that Being is one and the same as well, meaning that beings would show up the same way or have the same meaning at all times and places.

But *Dasein* is always pluralized by time and place. Thus Being is pluralized as well, meaning that beings show up in different ways and have different meanings in different times and places. Traditional philosophy seeks an objective, cosmopolitan "view from nowhere." Heidegger's *Dasein* is a view from somewhere. But *Dasein* is not to be understood as the isolated individual, for beings show up to us in terms of *shared* meanings, i.e., languages and cultural practices.

BEING & CULTURE

I want to conclude by saying a few words about the relationship of Being and culture. Heidegger holds that Being is the interplay of presence and absence through which beings show up to the knower, *Dasein*. The element of presence in Being consists simply of any form of direct awareness. The element of absence is any cognitive commerce with beings in their absence.

Heidegger held that our capacity to deal with beings in their absence is grounded in the faculties of memory and imagination, in language, and in the various meaningful practices and attitudes that make up a culture. Our culturally rooted attitudes and practices are an absolutely crucial element in our experience of the world.

One of the first things that one notices about a different culture is its different attitudes toward space and time. All human societies have a sense of the appropriate personal space that each person occupies and that cannot be transgressed without some sort of violation of propriety. All cultures also have their own characteristic perceptions of time. Cultures with cyclical conceptions of time tend to be extremely conservative and also very close to and rooted in nature. Such cultures are less likely to regard change as progress and more likely to regard it as degeneration and eccentricity. Cultures with linear conceptions of time are much more comfortable with change and liable to describe it as progress rather than decay or eccentricity. Some cultures take things at a more leisurely pace than others.

These different cultural attitudes and characteristic practices allow the world to show up in different ways. Thus, when we take a culture as a whole — looking both at its characteristic practices and attitudes and at the different ways they allow the world to show up to us — it is perfectly legitimate to identify Being and culture, and different cultures with different ways of Being.

Counter-Currents, March 5, 2015

HEIDEGGER'S QUESTION
BEYOND BEING

Everybody knows that Martin Heidegger was deeply interested in "Being," indeed obsessed with it. If Spinoza was the "God-intoxicated philosopher," Heidegger was surely the Being-intoxicated philosopher.

But this is not really true. Heidegger was not the least bit curious about what the word "Being" (the German "*Sein*") refers to. His concern, rather, was something "beyond" Being. Heidegger's concern was the "meaning" (*Sinn*) of Being. And the meaning of Being is something different from what the word "Being" refers to.

For Heidegger, "Being" is how beings (persons, places, things) *disclose* themselves, i.e., make themselves present, to a knower. The *meaning* of Being, by contrast, is how *Being* discloses itself to a knower. Being is the disclosure of beings. The meaning of Being is the disclosure of Being.

Heidegger claims that there is an "ontological difference" between Being and beings, i.e., a difference between *beings* and their *disclosure* (Being). The difference between *Being* and the *meaning of Being* is a "meta-ontological difference" between Being and its disclosure to us.

Ontology is the study of Being. And if there is a difference between Being and the meaning of Being, then studying the meaning of Being is something different from ontology. Many people mistake Heidegger for an ontologist, because they do not differentiate between Being and the meaning of Being. Indeed, the "meta-ontological" difference is ignored by most Heidegger scholars, Thomas Sheehan, Graeme Nicholson, Otto Pöggeler, and Mark Okrent being notable exceptions.[1]

---

[1] For explicit discussions of the meta-ontological difference, see Thomas Sheehan, "On Movement and the Destruction of Ontology," *The Monist* 64 (1981): 534–42; Graeme Nicholson, *Illustrations of Being: Drawing Upon Heidegger and Upon Metaphysics* (Atlantic Highlands,

1. THE "QUESTION OF BEING"

On page 1 of *Being and Time*, one finds the words: "Introduction. Exposition of the Question of the Meaning of Being [*Frage nach dem Sinn von Sein*]." This is followed by chapter 1, "Necessity, Structure, and Priority of the Question of Being [*Seinsfrage*]." And section one of that chapter is called "The necessity of an explicit recapitulation of the question of Being [*Frage nach dem Sein*]." Heidegger is not talking about three different questions here. The question of the *meaning* of being is the same as the "*Seinsfrage*"; it is the same as the "*Frage nach dem Sein*."

A natural interpretation is that the question of the meaning of Being is about what the word "Being" *refers* to, namely Being. On this reading, then Heidegger is simply an ontologist. "The question of the *meaning* of Being," is simply a long-winded way of saying "the question of Being" (the "*Seinsfrage*" or "*Frage nach dem Sein*"). All three questions are asking about the phenomenon to which the word "Being" refers.

But it is dangerous to assume that when philosophers speak of the "sense" (*Sinn*) of a word they mean what the word *refers to*, i.e., its "referent." *Sense* and *reference* are two different things. For instance, Gottlob Frege was famous for pointing out that the "morning star" and "evening star" *refer* to the same thing, namely the planet Venus. But "morning star" and "evening star" don't have the same *sense*. Thus there is more to a word's meaning than what it refers to. To be clear, I am not claiming that Heidegger was *influenced* by Frege. But Heidegger was deeply influenced by Husserl, and, as we shall see, Husserl's phenomenology does not reduce sense to reference either.

2. "THE BASIC QUESTION OF BEING ITSELF"

In a September 1946 text, "The Basic Question of Being Itself," dictated by Heidegger to Jean Beaufret, Heidegger makes clear

---

N.J.: Humanities Press, 1992), pp. 98–106; Otto Pöggeler, "Heidegger's Topology of Being," in Joseph J. Kockelmans, ed., *On Heidegger and Language* (Evanston: Northwestern University Press, 1972); and Mark B. Okrent, "The Truth of Being and the History of Philosophy," in Hubert L. Dreyfus and Harrison Hall, eds., *Heidegger: A Critical Reader* (Oxford: Blackwell, 1992).

the essentially *meaning-oriented* nature of his quest and how it differs from classical ontology.[2]

> On the basis of my own philosophical formation, which began already in the Gymnasium as I worked on Aristotle . . . the question *ti to on* [What is Being?] has become for me the guiding question of philosophy.[3]

Here is the Heidegger that everyone knows, the Heidegger asking about Being. The next paragraph, however, introduces several distinctions.

> I recognized one day that at the beginning of Western philosophy, and consequently in the entirety of subsequent philosophy, the question "What are beings as such?" [Was ist das Seiende als solches?] is the guiding question.[4]

Here Heidegger sets out the question of traditional ontology: "What are beings—beings (*Seiende*), not Being (*Sein*)—as such?" The answer to the question "What are beings as such?" is, of course, Being. Traditional ontological inquiry is, then, directed at Being. Traditional ontological inquiry is trying to give an account of Being—Being as the Being of beings. Traditional ontological inquiry is after what the word "Being" refers to.

---

[2] Martin Heidegger, "Die Grundfrage nach dem Sein selbst" (henceforth cited as GF), *Heidegger Studies* 2 (1986): 1–3. In English: "The Basic Question of Being as Such" (henceforth cited as BQ), trans. Parvis Emad and Kenneth Maly, *Heidegger Studies* 2 (1986): 4–6. This text not only displays the meta-ontological difference between Being and the meaning of Being, it also admirably displays the unity of Heidegger's philosophical career—as opposed to the overly neat "Heidegger I" and "Heidegger II" division. David Krell reports that Heidegger thought that it would take "about 100 years" for scholars to get beyond this interpretation. We could try harder. See David Farrell Krell, "Work Sessions with Martin Heidegger," *Philosophy Today* 26 (1982): 126–38, p. 134.

[3] GF, p. 1; BQ, p. 4.

[4] GF, p. 1; BQ, p. 4.

"But," Heidegger continues:

a second question was never raised: "What is Being [*Sein*] itself, and wherein is the manifestness of Being itself and its relation to man grounded, and in what does the manifestness of Being and its relation to man consist?"[5]

First, Heidegger distinguishes the traditional ontological question of the Being of beings from his question of "Being itself." Heidegger also calls this latter question the question of "Being as Being." But what does it mean to think "Being itself"? Does it mean thinking Being alone, without any relation to anything other than itself, without relation to any horizon or context? Of what would such a thinking consist? Would it be some sort of unmediated intuition?

Heidegger's first attempt to think the meaning of Being, in *Being and Time*, still treated the meaning of Being in relation to a particular being, *Dasein*. Heidegger's turn from exploring the meaning of Being in relation to *Dasein* to exploring the meaning of Being in relation to "Being itself" or "Being without beings" is usually called the "turn" (*Kehre*) in Heidegger's thought.

David Farrell Krell reports being puzzled by the turn and "disturbed by that expression 'Being without beings.' If we set off to encounter Being itself without recourse to *ta onta* [beings], what is to prevent our reenacting the play of metaphysics, but this time as sheer farce?"[6] When he raised this problem with Heidegger, Heidegger's answer was:

You must remember that the attempt to think Being without reference to beings is always historical; that is to say, Being takes on varied significance in the different epochs of the history or sending of Being. That is what it means to think Being without beings.[7]

---

[5] GF, p. 1; BQ, p. 4.
[6] Krell, "Work Sessions with Martin Heidegger," p. 135.
[7] Quoted in Krell, "Work Sessions with Martin Heidegger," p. 135.

The purpose of Heidegger's turn from *Dasein* to Being itself was not, then, the attempt to think about the meaning of Being without reference to any context. Rather, Heidegger's purpose was to *change* the context from *Dasein* to the history of ontology.

Heidegger's second question—namely, "What is the manifestness of Being itself?"—introduces the "meta-ontological" difference between Being and the meaning of Being. Heidegger makes clear the identification of the meaning of Being with the manifestness (*Offenbarkeit*) of Being in the following passage, which also identifies the meaning and the manifestness of Being with the "clearing" (*Lichtung*) of Being and with what is fundamental in "fundamental ontology," i.e., the foundation for traditional ontology.

> . . . insofar as *Being and Time* deals with ontology, it is dealing with fundamental ontology, which—to put it in traditional terms—is concerned with founding an ontology as such and thus with founding a general ontology. Strictly speaking, this question is no longer an ontological question at all, if ontology is understood as the general and special enquiry into the Being of beings and their realms—our question is no longer concerned with the Being of a being [that is: with the referent of the term "Being"].[8]

Here Heidegger distinguishes traditional ontology, which deals with the phenomenon of Being, and fundamental ontology. He then goes on to characterize the question of fundamental ontology as the inquiry into the meaning of Being.

> To put it more clearly, this question is no longer concerned with a being in respect to its Being, whose "meaning" [*Sinn*] as such is taken for granted, already established, and never questioned anywhere, from Parmenides up to Nietzsche. Rather the question concerning Being as such—concerning the manifestness and clearing [*Offenbarkeit und*

---

[8] GF, pp. 1–2; BQ, pp. 4–5, emphasis added.

Lichtung] of Being (not beings) — is the only question.[9]

Heidegger later adds another word for the object of fundamental ontology: unconcealment (*Unverborgenheit*):

> In *Being and Time* this question [the question of fundamental ontology] carries the title of the question concerning the *Sinn* of Being [*Frage nach dem Sinn von Sein*]. . . and we can say in short that "*Sinn*" . . . is the realm of unconcealment or clearing [*Unverborgenheit oder Lichtung*] (understandability [*Verstehbarkeit*]), wherein all understanding or projection (as bringing into the open [*in Offene bringen*]) is possible.[10]

Heidegger then adds yet another word: the truth (*Wahrheit*) of Being.

> In *Being and Time* the question has to do exclusively with the truth [*Wahrheit*] of Being and not with the Being of beings — thus it is no longer concerned with ontology, whether general or special.[11]

It is clear that Heidegger distinguishes between Being and the meaning of being, between ontology and fundamental ontology: on the one side, we have traditional ontology, which looks into a phenomenon known as the Being of beings. On the other side, we have fundamental ontology, which looks into something variously known as the meaning of Being, the manifestness of Being, the clearing of Being, the truth of Being, and the unconcealment of Being.

3. HUSSERL & HEIDEGGER ON BEING & CATEGORIAL INTUITION

Edmund Husserl helps us make sense of the distinction between the meaning of Being and what the word "Being" refers

---

[9] GF, p. 2; BQ, p. 5.
[10] GF, p. 2; BQ, p. 5.
[11] GF, p. 2; BQ, p. 5.

to in his Sixth *Logical Investigation*. In "The Basic Question of Being Itself," Heidegger writes:

> Only after encountering Husserl—whose writings I had already studied, of course, but had only read like other philosophical writings—did I develop a lively and fruitful relation to the real carrying out of phenomenological questioning and description.
>
> Only then could I develop philosophically the question that actually got me moving, namely the basic question concerning Being itself.[12]

Husserl, in short, helped Heidegger to formulate the meta-ontological distinction between the meaning of Being and the phenomenon of Being.

In his 1963 memoir "My Way to Phenomenology," Heidegger makes clear which of Husserl's works helped him to formulate the question of the meaning of Being: The Sixth *Logical Investigation*, specifically its discussion of the distinction between sensuous and categorial intuition.[13] Husserl thought that when we verify a proposition like "The paper is white" by looking at an actual piece of paper, we not only have a sensuous intuition of paper and its whiteness but also a "categorial" intuition of the "is." That is: The paper "shows up" as being articulated by acts of thinking that divide its whiteness from it, bring it into relief, and join it explicitly to it in the proposition. We move from a sheet of white paper to "paper taken as white" to "The paper is white," and with each thoughtful act, the intuitional fulfillment is altered and enriched as well.[14] For Husserl, the world actually

---

[12] GF, p. 1; BQ, p. 4.

[13] Martin Heidegger, "Mein Weg in die Phänomenologie," *Zur Sache Des Denkens* (henceforth cited as ZD) (Tübingen: Niemeyer, 1969), p. 86. In English: "My Way to Phenomenology," in *On Time and Being* (henceforth cited as TB), trans. Joan Stambaugh (New York: Harper & Row, 1972), p. 78.

[14] On categorial intuition, see Edmund Husserl, *Logical Investigations* (henceforth cited as LU), 2 vols., trans. J. N. Findlay (Atlantic Highlands, N.J.: Humanities Press, 1970), vol. 2, Investigation VI, esp.

looks different when we articulate it in thought. So when we verify a proposition, we don't just see the paper and its whiteness but we also somehow "see" the "isness" of the paper. In other words, we can somehow "see" *Being*.

At this point, many readers are probably baffled. In all candor, I find categorial intuition baffling too. Unlike most of Husserl's phenomenological exercises, this one does not seem "replicable." To my knowledge, I have never "intuited" the "isness" of worldly beings *alongside* their traits. I don't even know where to begin to try. It seems to overlook the distinction between worldly experience and philosophical reflection. But *Heidegger* thought it was a promising lead, so let's see where he goes with it.

The development of Heidegger's question of the meaning of Being through his engagement with Husserl's Sixth *Logical Investigation* is well-documented in Heidegger's 1925 Marburg lecture course, *History of the Concept of Time*.[15] In it, Heidegger offers a lengthy and sympathetic discussion of categorial intuition. In his important 1962 lecture "Time and Being," Heidegger alludes to the doctrine of categorial intuition in the Sixth Investigation.[16] And in his last seminar at Zähringen in 1973, Heidegger again explicitly named the doctrine of categorial intuition in the Sixth Investigation as crucial to the formulation of the question of the meaning of Being.[17]

Husserl's claim that the "is" can be categorically intuited in experience was the impetus to Heidegger's idea that Being can be investigated by phenomenology.[18] Heidegger's concept of

---

ch. 1, "Sensuous and Categorial Intuitions."

[15] Martin Heidegger, *History of the Concept of Time: Prolegomena*, trans. Theodore Kisiel (Bloomington: Indiana University Press, 1985).

[16] Martin Heidegger, "Zeit und Sein," in ZD, p. 3. In English: "Time and Being," in TB, p. 3.

[17] In Martin Heidegger, *Vier Seminare*, ed. Curd Ochwaldt (Frankfurt: Klostermann, 1977). In English: *Four Seminars*, trans. Andrew Mitchell and François Raffoul (Bloomington: Indiana University Press, 2003).

[18] See, for instance, the following articles: Robert Sokolowski, "Husserl's Concept of Categorial Intuition," in J. N. Mohanty, ed., *Phenomenology and the Human Sciences*, Supplement to *Philosophical Topics* 12

Being is not *just* categorial intuition. But Heidegger's understanding of Being *began* with categorial intuition. Then Heidegger expanded his conception of Being to include all the "phenomena of phenomenology," i.e., the disclosure of beings to a knower, *Dasein* (what Husserl called, in idealist language, "transcendental subjectivity"). This is, moreover, true throughout all of Heidegger's mature philosophical works, from *Being and Time* to his last writings. For instance, in the Introduction to *Being and Time*, Heidegger clearly identifies the Being of beings with the phenomenon studied by phenomenology:

> Phenomenology is our way of access to what is to be the theme of ontology, and it is our way of giving it demonstrative precision. Only as phenomenology, is ontology possible. In the phenomenological conception of "phenomenon" what one has in mind as that which shows itself is the Being of beings, its *Sinn*, its modifications and derivatives.[19]

(1981): 127–41; Richard Cobb-Stevens, "Being and Categorial Intuition," *The Review of Metaphysics* 44 (1990): 43–66; Theodore Kisiel, "Heidegger (1907–1927): The Transformation of the Categorial," in Hugh J. Silverman, John Sallis, and Thomas M. Seebohm, eds., *Continental Philosophy in America* (Pittsburgh: Duquesne University Press, 1983); Rudolf Bernet, "Husserl and Heidegger on Intentionality and Being," *Journal of the British Society for Phenomenology* 21 (1990): 136–52; Jacques Taminiaux, "Heidegger and Husserl's *Logical Investigations*: In Remembrance of Heidegger's Last Seminar (Zähringen, 1973)," in, *inter alia*, John Sallis, ed., *Radical Phenomenology: Essays in Honor of Martin Heidegger* (Atlantic Highlands, NJ: Humanities Press, 1978); and Jiro Watanabe, "Categorial Intuition and the Understanding of Being in Husserl and Heidegger," in John Sallis, ed., *Reading Heidegger: Commemorations* (Bloomington: Indiana University Press, 1993).

[19] Heidegger, *Sein und Zeit* (henceforth cited as SZ) (Tübingen: Niemeyer, 1986), p. 35; in English: *Being and Time* (henceforth cited as BT), trans. John Macquarrie and Edward Robinson (San Francisco: Harper, 1962), p. 60 and Introduction to *Being and Time*, trans. Joan Stambaugh, in Martin Heidegger, *Basic Writings* (henceforth cited as BW), ed. David Farrell Krell (San Francisco: Harper, 1977), p. 84.

Or: ". . . phenomena, understood phenomenologically, are always just what constitutes Being . . . ."[20] Or: ". . . phenomenology is the science of the Being of beings—ontology."[21]

If the Being of beings is identical to the phenomenon studied by phenomenology, the next question is: What is the phenomenon studied by phenomenology? Heidegger offers an answer in Kantian terms:

> If we remain within the horizon of the Kantian problematic, we can illustrate what is conceived phenomenologically as phenomenon, disregarding other differences, when we say that what already shows itself, though unthematically, in appearances prior to and always accompanying what we commonly understand as phenomena can be brought thematically to self-showing, and what thus shows itself in itself ("the forms of intuition") are the phenomena of phenomenology.[22]

In Kantian language, the phenomenon of phenomenology is the "a priori synthetic": the conditions for the possibility of experience that are always at work in allowing beings to show up to us, but that remain unnoticed because they direct our attention away from themselves and to the beings that they make present. But these conditions can become present when we reflectively disengage ourselves from the objects of first-order, worldly experience and turn our attention to the subject. Heidegger's example is the Kantian "forms of intuition," but he also could have mentioned the categories and the transcendental unity of apperception.

In Husserlian language, the phenomenon of phenomenology is transcendental subjectivity: the acts and structures of subjectivity that allow beings to become present. Described in more "objective" terms, the phenomenon of phenomenology is the presence (and the absence) of beings, as distinguished from the

---

[20] SZ, p. 37; BT, p. 61; BW, p. 85.
[21] SZ, p. 37; BT, p. 61; BW, p. 86.
[22] SZ, p. 31; BT, pp. 54–55; BW, p. 78.

beings that are present and absent.

Being for Heidegger is, therefore, what Kant called the transcendental conditions for the possibility of knowledge. Being, for Heidegger, is what Husserl called transcendental subjectivity. Or, as Thomas Prufer put it with gnomic precision, for Heidegger Being is "the presence/absence (taken as such) of the present/absent, that is, of that-which-is(-present/absent)."[23]

For Heidegger, Being is the interplay of presence/absence through which beings become present to a knower. Being is the interplay of presence and absence of beings to human beings—or, to be more precise, to *Dasein*, which Thomas Prufer calls "the dative of manifestation," the being "to whom" beings are given and for whom Being can become a question, i.e., the being who can reflect upon Being.[24] Heidegger's famed ontological differ-

---

[23] Thomas Prufer, "Husserl, Heidegger, Early and Late, and Aquinas," in *Recapitulations: Essays in Philosophy* (Washington, D.C.: The Catholic University of America Press, 1993), p. 83. Cf. the earlier version of this essay, "Heidegger, Early and Late, and Aquinas," in Robert Sokolowski, ed., *Edmund Husserl and the Phenomenological Tradition: Essays in Phenomenology* (Washington, D.C.: The Catholic University of America Press, 1989). On Being as presence/absence, see also Thomas Prufer, "Heidegger's Dasein and the Ontological Status of the Speaker of Philosophical Discourse," in John K. Ryan, ed., *Twentieth-Century Thinkers* (New York: Alba House, 1965). See also Thomas J. Sheehan, "On Movement and the Destruction of Ontology"; "On the Way to *Ereignis*: Heidegger's Interpretation of Physis," in Hugh J. Silverman, John Sallis, and Thomas M. Seebohm, eds., *Continental Philosophy in America* (Pittsburgh: Duquesne University Press, 1983); and "Nihilism, Facticity and Economized *Lethe*: A Reflection of Heidegger's *Zur Seinsfrage*," in *Heidegger: A Centennial Appraisal* (Pittsburgh: The Simon Silverman Phenomenology Center, 1990).

[24] In Prufer's language, *Dasein* is *materially* identical with human beings but not *formally* so; other beings that can question Being are at least conceivable. It is significant that Heidegger defines *Dasein* not as the being that "has" Being (i.e., that has beings present to it). This is true of all conscious beings—cats, dogs, mice, bugs, etc. What makes *Dasein* different from bugs is that *Dasein* not only has beings present to it, but also can reflect upon their presence. *Dasein* puts Being in question. *Dasein* can, furthermore, question the presence of presence

ence between Being and beings is the difference between the presence of a being and the being that is present. It is the difference between the absence of a being and the being that is absent.

Throughout his career, Heidegger does not depart from this identification of Being with the presence/absence interplay. For instance, in "The End of Philosophy and the Task of Thinking," Heidegger claims that Being, which is the matter (*Sache*) of philosophy is "the presence of that which is present" (*der Anwesenheit des Anwesenden*).[25] He equates the pair "Being and thinking" (*Sein und Denken*) with "presence and apprehending" (*Anwesenheit und Vernehmen*).[26] And he equates the meta-ontological question of "Being as Being" (*Sein als Sein*) with the question "how can there be presence as such [*Anwesenheit als solche*]."[27]

In sum: Heidegger's conception of the phenomenon of Being began with Husserlian categorial intuition and was soon expanded to include all of the phenomena of phenomenology. Heideggerian Being is the interplay of presence/absence. But this is not the whole truth. This interpretation coheres well with the conventional understanding of the question of Being: the question "To what does the word 'Being' refer?" And the answer is: the interplay of presence/absence. But Heidegger's primary focus is not Being but the *meaning* of Being, understood as different from Being, just as Being is different from beings.

4. HUSSERL ON EMPTY & FILLED INTENTIONS

Husserl's Sixth *Logical Investigation* throws considerable light on Heidegger's distinction between Being and the meaning of

---

itself, the meaning of Being. Were Heidegger's topic the referent of Being (namely, the presence of beings) rather than its meaning, he need not have interrogated *Dasein*. He could just as well have begun his investigation of Being with a preparatory fundamental analytic of "bug-sein."

[25] ZD, p. 73. In English: "The End of Philosophy and the Task of Thinking," trans. Joan Stambaugh, in BW, p. 386. Also in TB, p. 66.

[26] ZD, p. 75; TB, p. 69; BW, p. 387.

[27] ZD, p. 77; TB, p. 70; BW, p. 389.

Being. Husserl discusses categorial intuition in the Second Section, "Sense and Understanding."[28] The First Section, "Objectifying Intentions and their Fulfillments: Knowledge as a Synthesis of Fulfillments and its Gradations" presents knowledge as the synthesis of "empty" and "filled" intentions.[29]

The traditional understanding of intentionality is as a *real* relationship. On this account, to say that consciousness is always conscious of something is to say that, on the one hand, there is a subject, on the other hand, there is an object, and between them is an intentional relationship. One implication of this interpretation of intentionality is that, if the object is removed, the intentional relationship lapses. If intentionality is a real relationship, then it cannot survive without both relata. Subtract one or the other, and the intentional relationship vanishes.

This conclusion, however, creates problems. If there are no intentional states without objects, then what are we to make of names like "Xanadu," concepts like "the unicorn," phrases such as "the gold mountain," and propositions like "The present king of France is bald"? The hard-core naïve realist would be tempted simply to deny that they are meaningful. After all: if no referent, then no intentional relationship, then no meaning. But clearly these do have meaning. Any moderately literate native speaker knows what they mean, and it would be folly to deny it.

But how do we account for meaning without a real object? Are we to say that these concepts refer to "ideas in our heads"? This can't be so—simply because it isn't the case that when I talk about Xanadu, I am talking about an idea in my head. Rather, I am using an "idea in my head" to talk about Xanadu. If Xanadu is not, then, a place in the world or an idea in the head—if it is not an existent entity or a psychic entity—is it perhaps an ideal entity existing in some sort of third realm? This multiplication of posited entities has offended aesthetic sensibilities and

---

28 LU, vol. 2, pp. 771–834, esp. ch. 1, "Sensuous and Categorial Intuitions."

29 LU, vol. 2, pp. 673–770, esp. ch. 1, "Meaning-Intention and Meaning-Fulfillment."

drawn the wrath of logicians from Russell to Quine.[30]

Husserl's distinction between empty and filled intentions allows him to neatly sidestep these problems by denying their common premise: that intentionality is a real relationship. For Husserl, an intention is a determinate, object-directed cognitive act, but Husserl does not think that intentionality is a two-term relationship between a subject and an object in the world, a relationship that lapses once the object is removed. Rather, Husserl holds that intentional relationships persist whether an object is present or absent. Whereas the old-fashioned Aristotelian would hold that a given intentional relationship derives its determinacy solely from the determinations of the object apprehended and loses its determinacy when the object is subtracted, Husserl holds that intentional acts have determinate structures built right into them, so that we can have determinate intentional states without any objects.[31]

To intend an object emptily is to intend it in its absence. Consider the Lincoln Memorial. We all probably know what the Lincoln Memorial is, what it looks like, and where it is located. Hundreds of miles from the Memorial, we can recollect a trip to the Memorial, or we can plan to take one. We can talk about its history and meaning. We can ask questions about its construction and design. We can evaluate its aesthetic and architectural merits. We can take up all of these intentional stances toward the Memorial, even though it may be hundreds of miles away, in virtue of the fact that determinate intentional states can exist without the actual physical presence of the object intended. Empty intentions allow us to speak about absent objects.

Now, if we were to go to the Memorial our empty intentional

---

[30] See, for example, Bertrand Russell, "Descriptions," in, *inter alia*, *Meaning and Reference*, ed. A. W. Moore (Oxford: Oxford University Press, 1993), and W. V. O. Quine, "On What there Is," *Review of Metaphysics* 2 (1948): 21–32.

[31] Husserl's critique of the idea of intentionality as a real relationship may be found in ch. 2 of *Logical Investigations* V, "Consciousness as Intentional Experience." See LU, vol. II, pp. 552–63. An excellent discussion of this point may be found in Heidegger's *History of the Concept of Time*, pp. 29–32.

acts would be "filled," that is: They would be filled by the actual intuitive presence of the Memorial. Some of our expectations would be filled; others would be disappointed. Some of our claims would be verified; others would be falsified. A filled intention is simply an empty intention that has been filled by the intuitive presence of the object intended—or cancelled by the intuitive presence of an object other than the one intended. Husserl calls the fulfillment of empty intentions "identity synthesis."

The emptiness and filledness of intentions can vary along a number of axes. What counts as a filled intention in one context can be an empty intention in another.[32] For instance, if I try to think of someone's name, I am intending the name emptily; when I recall the name, my empty intention is fulfilled; when I use the name to call to mind its bearer, the name is an empty intention; when I see the bearer, the intention is filled.

The categorial forms and complexity of empty intentions also vary. They can be proper names, like Xanadu. They can be universals, like "unicorn." They can be phrases, like "the gold mountain." They can be propositions, like "The present king of France is bald." Or they can be scientific theories, paradigms, "background knowledge," interpretive frameworks, traditions, life-forms, cultures, or world-views.

Husserl holds that there is an *ontological priority* of empty intentions over filled intentions, though there need not always be a *chronological priority*. By an "ontological" priority, I mean that empty intentions do not need intuitive fulfillments to exist and to be what they are. A determinate empty intention can exist as an empty intention, without any need for intuitive fulfillment whatsoever. Words can mean things, even though they do not refer to anything real, psychic, or in a third realm. Husserl, in

---

[32] See *Logical Investigations* VI, chs. 3–5. For a number of examples of different kinds of empty and filled intentions, see Robert Sokolowski, *Husserlian Meditations: How Words Present Things* (Evanston: Northwestern University Press, 1974), pp. 18–19. According to *Husserlian Meditations*, p. 19, n1, Sokolowski's account draws primarily on Husserl's mature formulation of the relationship between empty and filled intentions in ch. 1 of his *Formal and Transcendental Logic*, trans. Dorion Cairns (The Hague: Nijhoff, 1969).

short, liberates semantics from the need to account for meaning in terms of reference.

Whereas empty intentions do not need intuitive fulfillments, intuitions can exist and be what they are *only* as the fulfillments or cancellations of empty intentions. For example, we can take a dog as a dog only in virtue of the prior possession of the concept of dog, which is a universal empty intention. Even when we encounter unfamiliar phenomena, we encounter them precisely as unfamiliar—i.e., as the cancellations of settled, habituated empty intentions.

While Husserl would agree with Kant that intuitions without concepts are blind, he would not fully agree with Kant's claim that concepts without intuitions are empty, for Kant thinks that this emptiness is a problem, but Husserl does not. "Yes," Husserl, would say, "concepts without intuitions are empty; they are empty intentions. But this is not a problem, for an intention can be empty and still exist determinately." This means that Xanadu, the unicorn, the Gold Mountain, and "The present King of France is bald" can exist as meaningful intentional states, yet not refer to anything real at all.

The distinction between empty and filled intentions corresponds exactly to the distinction between Being and the meaning of Being. The phenomenon of Being is a filled intention. The meaning of Being is an empty intention. Heidegger, significantly, devotes a good deal of attention to the distinction between empty and filled intentions in the *History of the Concept of Time*. As in the *Logical Investigations*, Heidegger's account of the synthesis of empty and filled intentions immediately precedes his discussion of categorial intuition.

Husserl's categorial intuition is what Heidegger understands to be the phenomenon of Being. Thus to say that Heidegger's concern is not the phenomenon of Being is to say that his concern is not with categorial intuition as such. If Heidegger's concern were solely with categorial intuition, then his treatment of Being would not be an advance on Husserl's. Heidegger's concern lies elsewhere. Husserl teaches that every intuition—categorial or otherwise—is the fulfillment of an empty intention. Again: the determinate empty intention is ontologically, if not temporally prior, to all intuitive fulfillments. Heidegger's question of the meaning of Being is, therefore: What is the empty intention that is fulfilled in categorial intuition? Thomas Sheehan, in surely one of the most important lines in the Heidegger literature, phrases the question of the meaning of Being as follows: "What is the nature of the empty intention that can be 'filled in' by Being? Or: What is the relative absence from out of which Being is disclosed as presence?"[33]

Husserl's categorial intuition is the *referent* of the word "Being." Heidegger's account of the empty intention fulfilled by categorial intuition is the *meaning* or *sense* (*Sinn*) of Being.

The answers that Heidegger gives to the question of the meaning of Being changed throughout his career.

In the writings of the 1920s, particularly *Being and Time*, the meaning of Being is the temporal nature of *Dasein*. Time is the horizon in which Being becomes present.

In the 1929 text "What Is Metaphysics?" Being is equated with the nothing, *das Nichts*, which is given through *Angst*. Thus *Angst* is the meaning of Being.[34]

In "On the Essence of Truth" the meaning of Being is renamed the truth (*Wahrheit*) of Being.[35]

As we have seen in "The Basic Question of Being Itself," in the late writings, the meaning of Being is also called the manifestness (*Offenbarkeit*) and unconcealment (*Unverborgenheit*) of Being.

In "Time and Being," the meaning of Being is identified with the "it" in "it gives being" (*Es gibt Sein*) that Heidegger hears not as "There is Being" but rather as "It gives Being" or "It evidences Being."[36] Heidegger hears the verb "*geben*" phenomenologically,

---

[33] Thomas J. Sheehan, "Heidegger's Philosophy of Mind," in Guttorm Fløistad, ed., *Contemporary Philosophy: A New Survey*, vol. 4, *Philosophy of Mind* (The Hague: Nijhoff, 1983), p. 292.

[34] Martin Heidegger, "Was ist Metaphysik?" in *Wegmarken* (Frankfurt: Klostermann, 1967). In English: "What Is Metaphysics?" trans. David Farrell Krell, in BW.

[35] Martin Heidegger, "Vom Wesen der Wahrheit," in *Wegmarken*. In English: "On the Essence of Truth," trans. John Sallis, in BW.

[36] Martin Heidegger, "Zeit und Sein," in ZD. In English, "Time

as "to make evident." And the "it" that gives Being is its meaning (*Sinn*). In "Time and Being," Heidegger names this "it" "*Ereignis*," the contingent and unpredictable "event" by which one dominant meaning or interpretation of Being is replaced with another.

Finally, "In the End of Philosophy and the Task of Thinking," the meaning of Being receives the loftiest of all names: *Lichtung*, clearing. A *Lichtung* is a clearing in the woods in which one can encounter beings. The *Lichtung* of Being is the clearing where one can encounter Being. As Heidegger puts it: "In that [*Lichtung*] rests possible radiance, that is, the possible presencing of presence itself [*Anwesen der Anwesenheit*]."[37] And: "The *Lichtung* grants . . . the possibility of the path to presence [*Anwesenheit*] and grants the possible presencing of presence itself [*Anwesen dieser selbst*]."[38]

Because Being (presence/absence) is always the presence/absence of beings, the *Lichtung* is also, mediately, the place in which all present and absent beings come to presence. In Heidegger's words, "The *Lichtung* is the open for all things present and absent."[39] The *Lichtung* is "that within which alone pure space and ecstatic time and everything present and absent in them have the place which gathers and protects everything."[40]

Heidegger, in short, gave many different answers to the question of the meaning of Being, but the question always remained one of meaning, a question beyond Being to that which makes Being present.

5. HEIDEGGER THE PHENOMENOLOGIST

In "The Basic Question of Being Itself," Heidegger claims that "With that question [the question of the meaning of Being] I have always—and from the very beginning—remained outside the philosophical position of Husserl, in the sense of a transcen-

---

and Being," trans. Joan Stambaugh, in TB.

[37] ZD, p. 75; TB, p. 68; BW, p. 387.

[38] ZD, p. 75; TB, p. 68; BW, p. 387.

[39] ZD, p. 72; TB, p. 65; BW, p. 384.

[40] ZD, p. 73; TB, p. 66; BW, p. 385.

dental philosophy of consciousness"[41] In "The End of Philosophy and the Task of Thinking," Heidegger claims that "Hegel also, as little as Husserl, as little as all metaphysics, does not ask about Being as Being, that is, does not raise the question of how there can be presence as such"[42] Heidegger claims to go beyond Husserl by raising a question that Husserl never raised: the question of the meaning of Being.

But Heidegger does not truly go beyond Husserl, for two reasons, one methodological, the other substantive.

First, the meaning of Being is that which makes Being present. Present to whom? Meaningful to whom? Presence and meaning require a "to whom," a dative, a receiver of presence. In Husserl's terms, the dative is transcendental subjectivity. In the early Heidegger's terms, the dative is *Dasein*. Heidegger, then, is doing transcendental phenomenology from the beginning of his career to the end—although in his later writings he systematically obscures the "to whom" of manifestation.

Second, Heidegger is simply wrong to say that Husserl does not raise the question of the meaning of Being, for in his writings on internal time-consciousness, Husserl speaks of something called the "absolute time-constituting flow" of consciousness. The absolute flow is a level of consciousness more primordial than the transcendental ego and its bundle of intentional acts. It provides the "clearing" in which both transcendental subjectivity and the objects made present through transcendental subjectivity come to presence. Finally, the absolute flow accounts for the conditions for the possibility of transcendental reflection itself.[43]

Heidegger remained a phenomenologist to the end. Where

---

[41] GF, p. 1; BQ, p. 4.

[42] ZD, p. 77; TB, p. 70; BW, p. 389.

[43] See Edmund Husserl, *Zur Phänomenologie des inneren Zeitbewußt-seins* (1893–1917), ed. Rudolf Boehm (The Hague: Martinus Nijhoff, 1966); in English: *On the Phenomenology of the Consciousness of Internal Time* (1893–1917), trans. John Barnett Brough (Dordrecht: Kluwer Academic Publishers, 1991). On absolute consciousness in relation to Heidegger's project, see Prufer's "Husserl, Heidegger, Early and Late, and Aquinas."

Heidegger writes "Being" substitute "meaning." The "Being of beings" means the "meaning of beings to a knower." The "meaning of Being" means the "meaning of meaning to a knower." For Heidegger, ontology is really what is usually called epistemology, i.e., the theory of knowledge. Heidegger's "history of Being" is a reflection on the history of theories of knowledge. Heidegger's final word on the transformations of meaning, and of the meaning of meaning, over the history of Western philosophy is that it is ruled by inscrutable contingency.

If the trajectory of traditional metaphysics—e.g., Platonism and Aristotelianism—is toward intelligible, necessary being that exists independent of human consciousness, Heidegger's trajectory is in the exact opposite direction: toward mind-dependent meanings ruled by inscrutable contingency. Frankly, Heidegger's insistence on cloaking what is essentially a kind of epistemological anarchism in the language of ontology strikes me as perverse and even a bit fraudulent. Of course that does not alter the substance of his achievements as a phenomenologist. But those achievements will be better understood and appreciated once Heidegger the ontologist is unmasked.

Counter-Currents, October 29, 2014

MAKING SENSE OF HEIDEGGER

Thomas Sheehan
Making Sense of Heidegger: A Paradigm Shift
New York: Rowman & Littlefield, 2014

Making sense of Heidegger just got a whole lot easier.

When I was in graduate school, Aristotle and Heidegger were the two philosophers I studied most thoroughly. Heidegger is a notoriously difficult writer, so naturally I sought out secondary literature for guidance. Unfortunately, most Heidegger literature is not particularly helpful. The best guides to Heidegger I discovered were Otto Pöggeler, Graeme Nicholson, Michael Zimmerman, Theodore Kisiel, and Thomas Sheehan—especially Sheehan.[1]

Sheehan's work was particularly important for me, because he pays special attention to Heidegger's debts to Aristotle and Husserl, debts that cannot be overestimated but are usually given short shrift. I found Sheehan's writing to be so penetrating, while at the same time clear and engaging, that I went on to read practically everything he wrote, for instance his books *Karl Rahner: The Philosophical Foundations* and *The First Coming: How the Kingdom of God Became Christianity*, which I never would have read for the subject matter alone.[2]

Two of Sheehan's articles were particularly fateful for my

---

[1] See Otto Pöggeler, *Martin Heidegger's Path of Thinking*, trans. Daniel Magurshak and Sigmund Barber (Atlantic Highlands, N.J.: Humanities Press, 1989); Graeme Nicholson, *Illustrations of Being: Drawing Upon Heidegger and Upon Metaphysics* (Atlantic Highlands, N.J.: Humanities Press, 1992); Michael Zimmerman, *Heidegger's Confrontation with Modernity: Technology, Politics, Art* (Bloomington: Indiana University Press, 1990); and Theodore Kisiel, *The Genesis of Heidegger's Being and Time* (Berkeley: University of California Press, 1993).

[2] Thomas J. Sheehan, *Karl Rahner: The Philosophical Foundations* (Athens: Ohio University Press, 1987) and *The First Coming: How the Kingdom of God Became Christianity* (New York: Random House, 1986).

subsequent intellectual development, for he was the first person I ever read who mentioned Julius Evola and Alain de Benoist,[3] although my ultimate reactions were certainly not what he was aiming for.

Once I was out of graduate school, however, I stopped following the secondary literature on Heidegger, even the really good stuff. By then, I could read Heidegger on my own, without training wheels. And since I was a mere "amateur" Heideggerian, I had no professional credentials to maintain.

Of course I continued to follow new releases of Heidegger's own writings. And I admit to picking up a few pieces of secondary literature: Richard Polt's *Heidegger: An Introduction* and *The Emergency of Being*, Charles Bambach's *Heidegger's Roots: Nietzsche, National Socialism, and the Greeks*, Julian Young's *Heidegger's Later Philosophy*, and, just for the fun of it, Adam Sharr's *Heidegger's Hut*.[4] But I was pretty much on the wagon until November of 2014, when I decided to review Alexander Dugin's dreadful book on Heidegger.[5]

Fortunately, when I bought Dugin, Amazon suggested I might also like Thomas Sheehan's *Making Sense of Heidegger*. Never have I clicked a "buy" button more quickly. The book arrived as soon as it was published, actually on the day I finished reading Dugin. But still, it felt late, decades late. I wish Sheehan had published this book twenty-five years ago.

---

[3] Thomas J. Sheehan, "*Diventare Dio*: Evola, Nietzsche, and Heidegger," *Stanford Italian Review*, 20 (December, 1986): 279–92 and "Myth and Violence: The Fascism of Julius Evola and Alain de Benoist," *Social Research*, 48, 1 (Spring, 1981): 45–73.

[4] Richard Polt, *Heidegger: An Introduction* (Ithaca: Cornell University Press, 1999); Richard Polt, *The Emergency of Being: On Heidegger's "Contributions to Philosophy"* (Ithaca: Cornell University Press, 2006); Charles Bambach, *Heidegger's Roots: Nietzsche, National Socialism, and the Greeks* (Ithaca: Cornell University Press, 2003); Julian Young, *Heidegger's Later Philosophy* (Cambridge: Cambridge University Press, 2002); and Adam Sharr, *Heidegger's Hut* (Cambridge: MIT Press, 2006).

[5] See my "Dugin on Heidegger," below.

A PARADIGM SHIFT

Making Sense of Heidegger argues for a "paradigm shift" in Heidegger interpretation: from Being to meaning, and from meaning to the source of meaning. According to Sheehan, Heidegger's ultimate concern is with the question: What makes meaning possible? What makes it possible for beings to be meaningfully present to a knower? (For Heidegger, a scientific account of how the sense organs and the brain operate is not an adequate answer to this question, because science presupposes the meaningful presence of eyeballs, gray matter, etc.)

Sheehan makes a crushingly convincing case for his thesis, marshaling quotes from the nearly 100 volumes of Heidegger's published writings, analyzing Heidegger's basic terminology, establishing equivalencies among his terms, establishing equivalencies between Heideggerese and more intelligible idioms, re-translating and paraphrasing difficult texts in light of his analysis, and laying it all out step-by-step, with summaries and repetitions along the way, so you never lose the thread of the argument.

As you will see from some of the quotes below, Sheehan's prose can be dense, bristling with hyphenated phrases, neologisms and unfamiliar terms, and words and phrases in German, Latin, and untransliterated ancient Greek. It is a lot more forbidding and thorny than it needs to be, which artificially limits the audience and impact of Sheehan's argument to professional scholars and educated, dedicated amateurs. I wish that Sheehan's editors had forced him through one more draft with an eye to making this book intelligible to bright undergraduate students, which would have been possible for a writer of his proven skill. But still, the book is clear "in itself" and, unlike most literature on Heidegger, actually worth the effort. Heidegger is yet to find his Alan Watts, but whoever he may be will have to read this book.

Sheehan's book has ten chapters in three parts plus an Introduction and a Conclusion, occupying 294 pages altogether, plus three short appendices, a long and detailed bibliography of Heidegger's writings in German and English translations, a briefer biography of other works cited, and two indexes: one of

German, English, and Latin terms, the other of ancient Greek terms.

SHEEHAN'S THESIS

Sheehan states his basic thesis in his Foreword and Introduction (chapter 1) entitled "Getting to the Topic."

Heidegger is famously interested in "Being" (*Sein*). Yet Sheehan argues that Heidegger's concept of Being has been systematically misunderstood by most Heidegger scholars. In the philosophical tradition, talk of Being refers to objective, mind-independent reality, indeed "ultimate" reality—such as God, or atoms in void, or an underlying mental or material "stuff"—that gives rise to the beings we perceive around us.

For Heidegger, however, "Being" refers to the *meaningful presence* of beings to a knower. Heidegger makes this understanding quite explicit in "The End of Philosophy and the Task of Thinking" where he glosses "the Being of beings" as "the presence of that which is present."[6] Present to whom? Heidegger calls the one to whom beings show up *Dasein*. (In ordinary German, "*Dasein*" means existence. Heidegger treats it as a compound of *Da* [there] and *Sein* [Being], hence "the place of Being," i.e., the one to whom beings are present.)

Heidegger does not question the existence of mind-independent objects, although he was certainly skeptical of accounts of "ultimate" mind-independent realities. But for Heidegger, Being is ultimately involved with the human knower. Indeed, it always has been. One of the most remarkable features of Heidegger's interpretations of Parmenides, Heraclitus, Plato, and Aristotle are his arguments that even their accounts of Being are implicitly cast in relation to the human knower.

For Heidegger, then, Being = the meaningful presence of be-

---

[6] Martin Heidegger, "The End of Philosophy and the Task of Thinking," translated by Joan Stambaugh, in *On Time and Being*, trans. Joan Stambaugh (New York: Harper & Row, 1972), p. 62 and *Basic Writings*, revised and expanded, ed. David Farrell Krell (New York: HarperCollins, 1993), p. 438.

ings to man. Thus *ontology* (the branch of metaphysics that deals with Being) is equivalent to *phenomenology*, which studies the disclosure of beings to man.

But this is just the beginning of Sheehan's paradigm shift, for Heidegger's ultimate concern is not Being (understood phenomenologically) but something *beyond* Being. In *Being and Time*, Heidegger calls this the "sense" (*Sinn*) of Being (hence the title *Making Sense of Heidegger*). Heidegger has many other names for this something "beyond" Being: the temporality (*Zeitlichkeit*) of *Dasein*, the truth (*Wahrheit*) of Being, the essence (*Wesen*) of Being, Being itself or Being as such (*das Sein selbst*), the manifestness (*Offenbarkeit*) of Being, the clearing (*Lichtung*) of Being, the event of appropriation (*Ereignis*), etc.

For Sheehan, all of these names point to the same topic: *the source of meaningful presence*, that which opens up the "space" in which beings are meaningfully present to a knower. "The single issue that drove Heidegger's work was not being-as-meaningful-presence but rather the source or origin of such meaningful presence" (p. xv).

In Sheehan's terms, this source is the "thrownness" (*Geworfenheit*) or "thrown openness" (*der geworfener Entwurf*) of *Dasein*, to use the language of *Being and Time*. Or it is the "clearing" (*Lichtung*) or "appropriated clearing" (*die ereignete Lichtung*) of the later Heidegger. But both vocabularies refer to the same thing: the *a priori* (always-already-operative) conditions that make possible meaningful presence to a knower. "The always-already-operative thrown-open clearing is the 'thing itself' of all Heidegger's work" (p. 21). So I do not wear out the hyphen key on my computer, I am just going to boil this all down to one word: the clearing.

Before we go any further, I need to define the clearing (*Lichtung*) and another key term of Heideggerese: appropriation (*Ereignis*).

THE CLEARING

In ordinary German, *Lichtung* means "clearing," like a clearing in the forest. The verb *lichten* means to clear land. Although *Lichtung* is not derived from the word *Licht* (light), a clearing

does allow light to reach the forest floor and illuminate whatever enters the clearing. ("Light from above" is the literal
meaning of "epiphany." The clearing allows light from above.)
Heidegger uses the metaphor of the clearing to refer to the
conditions that allow beings to be meaningfully present to a
knower. The clearing is the "space" in which beings become
present.

We can see and hear physical objects in physical space. We
can see and hear them, because there is a space between them
and us that our senses can traverse. Physically, light and sound
come to us, but from the first-person point of view, our eyes
and ears reach out for experience.

Just as we see and hear things in physical space, Heidegger
believes that things have *meaning* in a "space" as well. Because
Heidegger is talking about meaning, not seeing, this use of
clearing exploits another sense of *lichten*: to weigh anchor, to
lighten a load, to free up. In this sense, *Lichtung* is a free and
open space: the space in which beings can be meaningfully encountered.

Each object has meaning within a larger network or "world"
of meanings supplied by language, culture, and tradition.
Worlds of meaning are collective. In hermeneutics, such con-
texts of meaning are called "horizons," for just as the horizon is
the boundary of the visible world, horizons are the context in
which things have meaning. But what *opens up* these horizons,
these worlds of meaning?

In *Being and Time*, Heidegger speaks of man as *Dasein*, the
place (*Da*) of meaning (*Sein*), and man is opened up as the
space of meaning by "temporality" (*Zeitlichkeit*), the temporal
structure of our consciousness of meaning. This is the sense in
which for Heidegger "time" is the "horizon" of "Being" (meaning). In his later writings, summarized in the 1962 lecture
"Time and Being," Heidegger offers new terms. Instead of Being, he speaks of (meaningful) presence (*Anwesenheit*). Instead
of time as the horizon of Being, he speaks simply of the clearing in which beings become meaningfully present.

For Heidegger, the clearing is intrinsically hidden. As
Sheehan puts it, quoting Heidegger at the end:

As the ultimate presupposition, the clearing must always be presupposed in any attempt to know it. It always lies "behind" us, so to speak, and it will always remain behind us (i.e., unknowable) even when we turn around to take a look at it. Consequently, we cannot go "beyond" or "behind" it without contradicting ourselves. We cannot (without moving in a vicious circle) seek the presupposition of this ultimate presupposition of all our seeking. "There is nothing else to which appropriation could be led back or in terms of which it could be explained." (p. 227)

Heidegger's term for the intrinsic hiddenness of the clearing is *Seinsvergessenheit* (forgottenness or oblivion of Being), although what is forgotten is not Being but the clearing, and it has not been forgotten so much as it has been hidden and overlooked throughout the history of Western philosophy.

APPROPRIATION

For Heidegger, *Ereignis* refers to the intimate and reciprocal relationship of man and meaning: meaning cannot exist without man, and man cannot exist without meaning.

In ordinary German, *Ereignis* means "event." However, from its first appearance as a technical term in Heidegger's lectures in 1919, it means more than an event. Contrary to Sheehan, who insists *Ereignis* does not mean an event *at all*, Heidegger introduces the term in the context of talking about processes of consciousness and "lived experience" (*Erlebnis*, which he hyphenates as *Er-lebnis* to intensify the sense of process). For Heidegger, *Ereignis* is the name of a more intimate connection between knower and known than *Er-lebnis*. To emphasize this intimacy, this mutual belonging between knower and known, Heidegger introduces a hyphen (*Er-eignis*), turning it—against all etymology—into a compound term meaning "to make one's own," to take possession. Heidegger later approved the French *appropriement* (appropriation, as in taking possession) as a translation of *Ereignis*. For Heidegger, the appropriation of man and meaning is mutual and reciprocal: we belong to one another.

The sense in which *Ereignis* also means "event" has to do with what Heidegger calls *Seinsgeschichte*, which is his account of the emergence of different worlds of meaning (such as the modern world, which is defined by the presupposition that all beings are transparent to consciousness and available for manipulation). Heidegger claims, in his late essay "Time and Being," that these ages simply happen, one after another, and since these ages set the outward boundaries of intelligibility, we cannot get behind their succession to understand their why and wherefore. Meaning happens. Worlds of meaning happen. We can make sense of things within these worlds of meaning. But we cannot make sense of meaning itself. What gives meaning is hidden behind its gift.

These collective worlds of meaning are created and sustained by man, but they are not created by human consciousness. (There is more to man than consciousness. Even within the mind, consciousness is just the tip of the iceberg.) For Heidegger, language, culture, and traditions *create* human consciousness; human consciousness does not create language, culture, and tradition. Human consciousness and creativity take place only within a space opened by language, culture, and tradition.

Heidegger does not deny that Shakespeare wrote plays, Handel wrote oratorios, and Klee painted pictures. But he would deny that their creations are entirely individual and entirely products of the conscious mind. If they were, they would be contrived and probably unintelligible. Human creativity is situated in existing worlds of meaning and traditions of practice, and it carries these forward. Humans are not disembodied consciousnesses who can create *ex nihilo*.

Thus when it comes to explaining deep historical transformations, Heidegger does not think that philosophers, poets, or other "hidden legislators" hatch ideas and plans and propagate them to the rest of the culture. Rather, he claims that such individuals are merely the first ones to become conscious of and articulate stirrings in the *Zeitgeist*.

This would seem obscurantist, were it not for the fact that it does capture our experience of being shaped and enthralled by collective worlds of meaning before we even attain self-awareness. It would seem disempowering, if it did not imply that dissenting ideas, too, are not merely the subjective dreams of marginal individuals but rather our awareness of historical forces far greater than ourselves. Perhaps dissent occurs to us only when change is already underway.

PART ONE: ARISTOTELIAN BEGINNINGS

In *What Is Called Thinking?* Heidegger recommends that his students spend ten or fifteen years studying Aristotle before they pick up Nietzsche. The same advice could apply to Heidegger himself. Thus Part One of Sheehan's book is called Aristotelian Beginnings, encompassing chapter 2, "Being in Aristotle," and chapter 3, "Heidegger Beyond Aristotle." These chapters focus on Aristotle, but they also pay sufficient attention to Heidegger's readings of Plato and the pre-Socratics to constitute a good introduction to Heidegger's interpretation of ancient philosophy.

The chapter on "Being in Aristotle" deals with Heidegger's reading of Aristotle as a proto-phenomenological thinker whose account of Being implicitly defines Being in relationship to the human knower: ". . . *ousia* [Being] is the intelligible appearance or meaningful presence (*aletheia* [truth] and *parousia* [presence]) of things in *logos*, and thus that *ousia* is the openness or availability of things to human beings" (p. 25). When Heidegger read Aristotle in light of Husserl's account of "categorial intuition" in the Sixth *Logical Investigation*, Heidegger was able to focus on the phenomenon of intelligible presence (as opposed to mere sense experience), which then led him to his own distinct question: What is the source of intelligible presence? This is the topic of chapter 3.

These chapters are a *tour de force*. They brought me back to my graduate seminars in Aristotle and rekindled my first feelings of astonishment at Aristotle's genius. Although this section is quite thorough and illuminating, at 76 pages, it becomes a bit of a slog. Sheehan himself suggests that some readers might be tempted to skip to the second section, on *Being and Time*, and read the Aristotle chapters later. I followed his advice, and I am glad I did. I think that he should have followed his own advice and made this the third and final section of the book.

Yes, one understands *Being and Time* better with a background in Aristotle, but that does not mean that we need to read about Heidegger's interpretation of Aristotle first. All of us read *Being and Time* first anyway. And we all had questions that were later clarified by understanding Heidegger's debts to Aristotle, Husserl, etc. Sheehan's order of exposition could have followed that path of discovery, and his book would have much more accessible for it.

A NEW LEVEL OF INQUIRY?

At the beginning of chapter 3, Sheehan argues that there are three levels to Heidegger's topic. According to Sheehan, Heidegger's ultimate topic is: (1) not Being (meaning), (2) not the meaning of Being (the meaning of meaning = the clearing), but (3) the meaning of the meaning of Being (the meaning of the meaning of meaning = the clearing of the clearing). In Sheehan's words:

> Heidegger's question turns out to be
>
> 1. not "Whence beings?" — the answer to that is: being; 2. nor even "Whence being at all?" — the answer to that is: the open clearing; 3. but rather "Whence and how is there 'the open'?" or equally "Whence and how is there the clearing?" (p. 69)

This is news to me.

Sheehan offers the following quote from Heidegger in support of this:

> When the being-question is understood and posed in this way, one must have already gone beyond being itself. Being and another now come into language. This "other" must then be that wherein being has its emergence and its openness (clearing—disclosing)—in fact, wherein

openness itself has its own emergence. (Heidegger, *Gesamtausgabe* vol. 73, part 1, p. 82, lines 20–24, translated in *Making Sense of Heidegger*, p. 69)

For Heidegger, the clearing is the ultimate condition of meaning. It is what makes everything else intelligible. And that means that it itself is not intelligible, meaning that we cannot place it in a wider context, i.e., a clearing of its own. If we could put it in a clearing of its own, then it would not, by that very fact, be the *ultimate* condition of meaning. This leaves us with two options.

1. First, one can accept that the clearing is unintelligible. Heidegger arrived at this conviction in 1930 in his lecture "On the Essence of Truth," in which he argued that the ultimate context of meaning cannot be made meaningful. As Sheehan puts it, "the clearing is intrinsically 'hidden': always present-and-operative but unknowable in its why and wherefore" (p. 116).
2. Second, one can claim that the clearing *makes itself* intelligible. And that is what Heidegger *seems* to be doing in the passage above: the "'other' . . . wherein being has its emergence and its openness (clearing—disclosing)" is our clearing. Then he claims that the clearing is "in fact, wherein openness itself [the clearing] has its own emergence."

Of course, if the clearing is entirely unintelligible, then everything Heidegger says about it is nonsense. It frequently *seems* that way, but it is not. This implies that something like the second position is true: We "encounter" the clearing "in" the clearing, and although we cannot "get behind" it to make "ultimate" sense of it, we can still say a lot about it. For one thing, we can talk about the functions it performs. For another thing, we can understand why we cannot understand it.

Sheehan interprets the passage from Heidegger quoted above as follows:

We note here again the two elements of Heidegger's own question (1) the move "beyond being" to its "whence" — namely, the clearing; and (2) the move "beyond the clearing" to *its* "whence" — namely *Ereignis* as the appropriation of ex-sistence. (p. 69)

I do not, however, think that *Ereignis* is "beyond the clearing" so much as it is a description from "within" the clearing of how the clearing operates, namely the clearing simply *happens*, and we can't get behind it to understand *why* it happens or *what* is causing it. *Ereignis* is another term for the basic inscrutability of the clearing.

PART TWO: THE EARLY HEIDEGGER

Part Two is divided into three chapters: chapter 4, "Phenomenology and the Formulation of the Question"; chapter 5, "Ex-sistence as Openness"; and chapter 6, "Becoming Our Openness."

The first chapter is a very accessible and engaging account of Heidegger's basic phenomenological approach to ontology: We are immersed in a world of meaning. The world is always-already meaningful, before we even try to make sense of it. For Heidegger, this world of meaning, this meaningful presence of beings to us (*Dasein*), is Being. Heidegger's overriding question is: What makes meaningful presence (Being) possible? What opens man up, allowing the meaningful presence of beings?

The second chapter deals with this question in terms of *Being and Time*, which aimed "to show that and how meaningful presence — 'being in general' — is made possible by and occurs only within human openedness as the clearing" (p. 134).

MAN'S OPENEDNESS

Heidegger distinguishes between individual instances of openedness, which he calls *Dasein*, and the structure of human openedness itself, which he calls *Existenz* and *Da-sein* (although he is not always consistent about using the hyphen). Sheehan renders the latter two terms as "ex-sistence," from the Latin *ex* + *sistere*, to be *forced* to stand ahead or beyond. This forced aspect is captured by "open*e*dness" as opposed to mere "openness."

On pp. 136–37, Sheehan points out an interesting quote from a posthumously published collection of 1941–42 notes,[7] where Heidegger claims that the "*Da*" in *Dasein* should not be translated as here, there, here/there, etc. (Which of course would include my preferred rendition "place.") Instead, Heidegger claims that the "*Da*" is not locative at all, but refers to the "openedness" of human ex-sistence. Of course, I do not think that anyone who translated the "*Da*" as here, there, etc. thinks it refers to a literal place, any more than the clearing is a literal clearing.

Sheehan gives a series of very interesting quotes from Heidegger on the "*Da*":

[The "*Da*"] should designate the openedness where things can be present for human beings, and human beings for themselves.

. . . being human, as such, is distinguished by the fact that to be, in its own unique way, is to be this openedness.

The human being occurs in such a way that he or she is the "*Da*," that is, the clearing of being. (p. 137)

The *Da* refers to that clearing in which things stand as a whole, in such a way that, in this *Da*, the being of open things shows itself and at the same time withdraws. To *be* this *Da* is a determination of man.

[Ex-sistence] *is* itself the clearing.

The clearing: the *Da* – *is* itself *ex-sistence*.

---

[7] Martin Heidegger, *Das Ereignis*, ed. Friedrich Wilhelm von Herrmann, Gesamtausgabe, vol. 71 (Frankfurt a.M.: Klostermann, 2009). In English: *The Event*, trans. Richard Rojcewicz (Bloomington: Indiana University Press, 2013).

The point is to experience *Da-sein* in the sense that human being itself is the *Da*, that is, the openedness of being, in that a person undertakes to preserve it, and in preserving it, to unfold it (See *Sein und Zeit*, p. 132f. [= 170f.]).

Ex-sistence must be understood as being-the-clearing. *Da* is specifically the word for the open expanse.

Ex-sistence [*das Da-sein*] is the way in which the open, the clearing, occurs, within which being as cleared is opened up to human understanding.

To be — the clearing — to be cast into the clearing as the open = to-be-the-*Da*. (p. 138)

Human ex-sistence means that man is not defined by what he is at present, what is simply there, what is simply actual, what shows up to an outside observer as a being occupying a delimited space at the present time. When we view human ex-sistence from the inside, we realize that to be human means to be *forced* outside the present, the actual, and into the future, the possible. This compulsion is what Heidegger means by "thrownness."

This thrownness outside the present and the actual is what makes man "open" to meaning. Humans ex-sist by projecting ahead of themselves a range of possibilities, a range of concrete potential ways of being. These possibilities are given to us by our past. They are also finite: We do not have all possibilities, and the possibilities that we do have cannot be simultaneously realized.

It is only in light of these possibilities that we "return" to what is present and actual and render it *meaningfully* present. For instance, if I look across the prairie and see an oncoming storm, I am "ahead of myself" in appraising what might happen, and in light of those possibilities, what is present shows up to me in terms of its serviceability for shelter or escape.

This temporal structure in which the past creates possibilities in terms of which we render things (past and present) as *meaningfully* present is the temporality (*Zeitlichkeit*) of *Da-sein*, which for Heidegger is the "horizon" of Being (meaning), i.e., that which opens man up, that which creates the space in which meaningful presence is possible. This temporal structure of being thrown into future possibilities and returning to render things meaningfully present is also the structure of *logos*. In *Being and Time*, Heidegger equates "the temporality [*Zeitlichkeit*] of discourse [*Rede* = *logos*]" with that of "*Dasein* [existence] as such" (quoted on p. 150).

Heidegger describes human ex-sistence by saying that "possibility is higher than actuality" and that human existence is a matter of "excess." Both of these claims point to the fact that human existence exceeds what is given and actual (to the outside observer). We exceed the actual and present into a realm of future possibilities.

On page 136, Sheehan makes a couple of dubious inferences from these claims.

First, that the priority of possibility over actuality is incompatible with a classical ethics of self-actualization, as if Plato and Aristotle did not recognize that each man has many possibilities besides the actualization of his nature in accordance with virtue; as if Aristotle believed, for example, that one can only hit the mean rather than stray into excess or defect.

Second, he claims that the idea of human ex-sistence being in "excess" of human actuality overturns the Greek idea of moderation (nothing in excess), as if the very notion of temperance did not imply the possibility of excess and defect in the pursuit of pleasure, and as if the very existence of human potentiality refutes the pursuit of virtue when in fact it is what makes it possible and necessary. Heidegger's "excess" is the space in which virtue, as well as the vices of excess and defect, become possible.

BECOMING WHO WE ARE

The third chapter of Part Two, "Becoming Our Openness," does extraordinary work in illuminating some of *Being and Time*'s most alluring yet elusive and obscure ideas, namely its existential and practical (but, as well shall see, not *moral*) dimension, which is encapsulated in the injunctions of the seventeenth-century German mystic Angelus Silesius, "Human being, become what you essentially are!" and of Pindar, "Become what you already are!"

Now, as a follower of the Platonic and Aristotelian idea of an ethics of self-actualization, I would interpret what we "already" or "essentially" are as our *daimon*, our ideal self, which exists in potency and whose actualization is the well-being (*eudaimonia*) we all seek.

Heidegger does not think we have a single determinate *daimon*, but a whole range of possibilities—possibilities that could include self-actualization but also self-betrayal, virtue as well as vice, good as well as evil. Thus the choice Heidegger is discussing is not the moral choice between good and evil, but the existential choice between embracing or rejecting our freedom. And for Heidegger, our freedom means a whole range of possibilities, not just the good ones.

But in what sense are we even faced with such a choice? Long before we are mature enough to reflect upon who we really are, people *tell* us who we are. These external spectators (the crowd) look upon us as actual, present beings and ascribe traits to us: jock, bimbo, nerd, preacher's kid, etc. Because we don't know better, we actually come to internalize these traits. But what are the chances that these descriptions actually fit, that they really capture who we are?

But before we can become who we really are—and as an Aristotelian, I think that is meaningful and possible—we need to embrace our freedom, meaning our whole range of possibilities, including the inevitability of our death and the possibility that we might die at any time, which gives a certain urgency to our mission.

"They" tell us that who we are. But when we look within, we discover that we are thrown ahead into a range of future possibilities. We are not what we are (right now), i.e., actuality. Rather, we are what we are not (yet), i.e., possibility. We are free either to accept the fact of our freedom, which is what Heidegger calls authenticity, or to flee it into inauthenticity, which basically boils down to shrugging off the burden of freedom and letting others determine our identity for us.

But what makes our freedom, such as it is, possible? Heidegger's answer would have to be: The things that *determine* us, which for him come down to our heritage: our language, culture, traditions, historical epoch, and the like. I would add our genetic heritage as well—our race, our sex, our individual traits—although that is a topic for another time. All of these give us certain possibilities, while making other things impossible. For example, being a prince or a peasant make certain things possible, other things impossible

And since it is in light of these possibilities that what is given becomes meaningfully present, our openedness as a whole is historically conditioned and particularized.

And if authenticity means embracing rather than fleeing our freedom, that is equivalent to embracing rather than fleeing from the heritage that determines us as well as frees us.

Heidegger talks about authentic *Dasein* "becoming its fate," but he might as well have said *amor fati*, for one can come to love our limits when one appreciates that they are the conditions of our freedom.

Heidegger's own discussion of our relationship to our past is primarily in terms of making our heritage *meaningfully present* in light of future possibilities, and retrieving/carrying forward certain elements. However, it strikes me that a deeper relationship with our past is implied by authenticity: not picking and choosing elements of our heritage that *show up* to us *within* our openedness, but embracing heritage as a *condition* of openedness—which, as an ultimate condition of intelligibility, remains obscure to us.

The affirmation of a form of historical identity so deeply constitutive of our self and self-consciousness that it can never be objectified, much less criticized or discarded, would place Heidegger in the tradition of anti-rationalist conservatism of David Hume and Edmund Burke. Sheehan—whose own Left-wing, progressivist agenda becomes more apparent as the book goes on—emphasizes the transcendental rather than the historical elements of Heidegger's account of openedness, and freedom rather than the boundaries that make it possible.

PART THREE: THE LATER HEIDEGGER

Part Three is divided into three chapters: chapter 7, "Transition: From *Being and Time* to the Hidden Clearing"; chapter 8, "Appropriation and the Turn"; and chapter 9, "The History of Being." The first two chapters can be discussed as a unit, because they deal with the same topic: Heidegger's concept of the "turn" (*Kehre*) which in its primary sense is identical to his concept of *Ereignis*.

One of Sheehan's most important accomplishments is his clarification of the multiple senses of Heidegger's "turn." The "turn" is usually thought of as a shift in Heidegger's thinking, either within *Being and Time* or between *Being and Time* and Heidegger's later thought. Sheehan argues, however, that the fundamental sense of the turn is identical to *Ereignis*, i.e., it refers to the mutual dependence of man and meaning: Meaning cannot exist without man, and man cannot exist without meaning.

The unity of man and meaning can, however, be viewed under different aspects: from the side of man or from the side of meaning. *Being and Time* was originally planned to have two divisions, each divided into three parts. In 1927, Heidegger published only parts 1 and 2 of division one. Part 3 was not published, and the manuscript was either lost or destroyed. Division two was never begun.

In *Being and Time*, parts 1 and 2, Heidegger approaches the man/meaning unity from the man side, using the phenomenological method to describe the temporal structure of existence, which opens the space of meaningful presence. In the unpublished part 3, Heidegger was to approach the same unity from the side of meaning. Instead of showing how man opens up the space of meaning, he was to show how the space of meaning claims man. As Heidegger put it, the first parts of *Being and Time* deal with "human being in relation to the clearing" while part 3 deals with "the clearing and its openness in relation to human being" (quoted in Sheehan, p. 244).

This shift in perspective is often misinterpreted as *the* turn in

Heidegger's thought. But it is intimately related to the primary sense of the turn: the unity of man/meaning, which allows us to look at it from either side.

Heidegger never published *Being and Time*, division one, part 3. Sheehan does an important service by gathering all the testimonies about the lost text to reconstruct its outline and contents, to speculate about its teaching, and to explain why it was never published.

In the 1930s, Heidegger's approach to his abiding topic — what makes meaningful presence possible — shifted from transcendental phenomenology to what he called *Seinsgeschichte*, which explores the different dispensations of Being/worlds of meaning in Western (and now world) history. This shift is also misinterpreted as *the* turn in Heidegger's thought.

However, this turn, like the other, is made possible by the primary sense of the turn. Indeed, the turn within *Being and Time* and the turn from *Being and Time* to the late Heidegger are attempts to execute the *same* shift of perspective: from a transcendental/human-sided approach to a historical/meaning-sided approach to the man/meaning unity. Why did the first turn fail, and why did the second take a historical form?

The first turn failed because every discourse requires a context. A phenomenology of human ex-sistence provided the context for the first parts of *Being and Time*, but when Heidegger set aside the transcendental phenomenological method and the human-centered standpoint, he needed another context, another standpoint, from which to explore the man/meaning relationship from the side of meaning. But he lacked this context at the time he was writing *Being and Time*.

In 1930, Heidegger came to the realization, discussed above, that if the clearing is the ultimate condition of meaning, it itself remains unintelligible. But, although one cannot get beyond the clearing, perhaps one can say something about it from inside. But how? The outline of *Being and Time*, division two — which was to be a dismantling of Western ontology, moving from Kant to Descartes to Aristotle — certainly provided a clue.

For Heidegger, meaning embodied in language, culture, and tradition constitutes human consciousness, not vice-versa. But to say more about how history shapes human consciousness, one would have to compare different historical epochs. Heidegger is not, however, interested in ordinary intellectual and cultural history, but in the succession of fundamental interpretive slants—the *a priori*, i.e., hidden and always-already-operative assumptions about the nature of man and world—that cut through and unify entire cultures and ages. This brings us to Sheehan's next chapter, "The History of Being," to which I will attend in due course.

INFLATING THE HUMAN

Heidegger's belief that socially embodied meaning constructs individual consciousness—i.e., that consciousness is not "behind" history but history is "behind" consciousness—is the substance of his "anti-humanism." "Anti-humanism" is something of a misnomer, though, since history and culture are just as "human" as individual consciousness. Heidegger is really opposed to the subject-centered transcendental method and the idea that the individual creates his own world of meaning, as opposed to receiving and passing on collective meanings to which he might contribute some small improvements.[8] The transcendental method also goes hand-in-hand with a dismissal of transcendent metaphysics. Sheehan writes:

> The paradox of *Being and Time* as published is that the *finitude* of ex-sistence guarantees the *infinitude* of ex-sistence's reach. Our structural engagement with meaning is radically open-ended and in principle without closure. Yes, there is an intrinsic limit to that stretch: ex-sistence can encounter the meaning only of material things, for as embodied and thrown, ex-sistence is "submitted" exclusively to sensible things rather than being open to trans-sensible ("meta-physical") reality. But that notwithstanding, the search for the meanings of spatio-temporal things meets no barrier inscribed "thus far and

---

[8] Even a Shakespeare's contributions to the English language are small compared to what he inherited.

no farther," because we can always ask "Why no farther? What am I being excluded from?" and thus transcend the barrier, if only interrogatively. And secondly, yes, ex-sistence is thoroughly mortal and will certainly die, and its death will mark the definitive end to its search for meaning. But although it will surely end, perhaps even tragically, ex-sistence will nonetheless go out with its glory intact, insofar as it will die *as* an in-principle unbounded capacity for the meaning of everything it can sensibly encounter. (p. 192)

First, it strikes me as vacuous to say that we can make sense of everything by stipulating that one of those "senses" includes awareness that we have not made sense of something. Second, if this notion of the Faustian infinitude of ex-sistence's reach is an accurate description of *Being and Time*, parts 1 and 2, it strikes me as precisely the kind of human-centric teaching that was to be modified by the turns in Heidegger's thinking within *Being and Time*, and from *Being and Time* to the later Heidegger.

Indeed, as Sheehan continues to set forth this Faustian interpretation of Heidegger, it looks suspiciously like what Heidegger came to call the "essence" of technology, i.e., the *a priori* assumption that all beings are in principle knowable and disposable by man:

Structurally and in principle we are *able* to know everything about everything, even though we never will. Such ever-unrealized omniscience comes with our very ex-sistence. (Husserl: "God is the '*infinitely distant man.*'") This open-ended possibility is a "bad infinity," which in this context denotes the asymptosis of endless progress in knowledge and control. Heidegger's philosophical critique of (as contrasted with his personal opinions about) the modern age of science and technology cannot, on principle be leveled against our ability to endlessly understand the meaning of things and even to bring them under our control, because this possibility is given *with* human nature, as Aristotle intimated and as Heidegger accepts in principle. What troubles Heidegger, rather, is the generalized overlooking of one's mortal thrown-openness in today's Western, and increasingly global, world. The mystery of human being consists in both the endless comprehensibility of whatever we can meet and the incomprehensibility of why everything is comprehensible. Everything is knowable — except the reason why everything is knowable. (p. 193)

The claim that we are able to "know everything about everything" strikes me as every bit as dogmatic as any claim of transcendent metaphysics. (Even if we knew everything about a particular subject, could we ever know *that* we knew everything?) And since when is "knowing" everything equivalent to "understanding the meaning" of everything, i.e., interpreting everything? Surely this kind of talk — which every academic knows can go on forever — is not necessarily equivalent to endless progress in knowledge.

Sheehan makes it quite clear that he thinks this Faustian viewpoint is not just "early Heidegger" but "late Heidegger" too. He also gives the strong impression that he thinks it is true:

. . . once Heidegger has established this argument about man's *a priori* projectedness, he can and must affirm the obvious: that within the limits of our thrownness, we ourselves do indeed decide the meanings of things on our *own* initiative, whether practically or theoretically. . . . Yes, we are structurally thrown-open; but nonetheless it is we ourselves, as existentiel actors, who decide the current whatness and howness of things, their *jeweiliges Sein*. What is more, there is *in principle no limit* to what we can know about the knowable or do with the doable. There should be no shrinking back from the human will, no looking askance at the scientific and technological achievements of existentiel "subjects" in the modern world . . . Underlying the whole of Heidegger's philosophy is the fact that we cannot encounter anything outside the parameters that define us as human — as a thrown-open, socially and historically embodied *logos*. But granted that much, we also cannot *not* make sense of anything we meet, whether in practice or in theory.... Heideggerians seem a bit anxious about the practical (not to mention technological) achievements of the existentiel subject—including socio-political projects for "changing the world." However, as *to zoon logon to echon* [living beings possessing reason] we possess the power not only to make sense of things cognitively but also to remake the world as we see fit, for better or worse. But we possess that power only because we are *possessed by* the existential ability to make sense and change the world . . . (pp. 208–209)

This sense of being "possessed" by the ability to know and do anything captures the enthralling quality of every dispensation of Being, including the *a priori* assumption of technological civilization, that Heidegger calls *Gestell* or *Ge-Stell*. (*Gestell* is another untranslatable bit of Heideggerese that means the *a priori* assumption that for man everything is transparent and available. This is the "essence" of technology, meaning the prevailing mode of disclosing beings that makes modern technological civilization possible.)

But whereas Sheehan thinks we should be celebrating this worldview, Heidegger sought to awaken us from it, to break the spell. How? By showing us that the idea that everything can be understood and controlled is itself an *Ereignis*, a dispensation of meaning that we cannot understand or control. And if we can't know *why* everything is knowable, isn't that a *refutation* of the idea that everything is knowable?

Sheehan himself says: "Everything is knowable—except the reason why everything is knowable," although he does not draw the conclusion Heidegger would like. If we cannot know *why* we think we can know everything, then we *cannot* know everything. Simply put, Heidegger is offering a counter-example to the idea we can know and control everything, and a single counter-example is sufficient to refute a universal generalization.

Heidegger's counter-example is not, moreover, just a single

instance that could be partitioned off as an exception to the rule, for what dispenses modernity is ultimately the whole of Western — and now global — civilization, understood as a realm of embodied meaning. We stand at the center of a circle — or better, a sphere — of meanings shading off into mysteries in all directions, and each time we bring a new mystery into the light, we understand that it is a gift from that which remains concealed.

DEFLATING THE TRANS-HUMAN

Sheehan's tendency to inflate the human (the subject-centered) is matched with a tendency to deflate the trans-human, historical dimensions of Heidegger's thought. This is particularly evident in his discussion of *Ereignis*. In keeping with his program of breaking us out of both the egocentrism of the phenomenological method and the vaulting ambitions of the *Gestell*, Heidegger speaks of *Ereignis* and the clearing almost as if they have wills of their own. Sheehan, however, dismisses this as merely "reifying" language that:

> . . . presents *Ereignis* or *Sein selbst* or *Seyn* as if it were a quasi-something that "catches sight" of human being, calls it into its presence, and makes it its own, as in such unfortunate sentences as . . . . "*Er-eignen* originally means: to bring something into view, that is, to catch sight of it, to call it into view, to ap-propriate it." The "something" that is allegedly "brought into view" is ex-sistence; and this hypostatizing language makes it seem that something separate from ex-sistence "sees" ex-sistence and makes it its own property. . . . The danger that constantly lurks in Heidegger's rich and suggestive lexicon is that his technical terms will take on a life of their own as words and then get substituted for what they are trying to indicate, the way some scholarship treats the clearing (or *das Sein selbst*) "as if it were something present 'over against' us as an object." Thus Heidegger's key term *Ereignis* — especially when English scholarship leaves it in the German — risks becoming a re-

ified thing in its own right, a supra-human Cosmic Something that enters into relations with ex-sistence, dominates it, and sends *Sein* to it while withholding itself in a preternatural realm of mystery. To avoid such traps and to appreciate what Heidegger means by *Ereignis,* we must always remember that the term bespeaks our thrown-openness as the groundless no-thing of being-in-the-world, which we can experience in dread or wonder. Above all we should apply Heidegger's strict phenomenological rule to appropriation itself: "avoid any ways of characterizing it that do not arise out of the personal claims it makes on you." (pp. 234–35)

But Heidegger's language does not suggest a false opposition between human ex-sistence and the clearing (which are just two different ways of viewing the same meaning). Instead, Heidegger is trying to articulate a real opposition between the individual ego and socially-embodied meaning. Heidegger is trying to communicate that meaning is not created by the individual ego, but instead the individual ego is created by socially-embodied meaning. When individuals reflect upon language, culture, and history, we experience them as things that existed before our consciousness emerged, as things that will continue to exist after our consciousness has ended, and as external forces that envelop and enthrall us. They do stand over against us as objects—and also behind us as conditions of our subjectivity. *Ereignis* is not a "supra-human Cosmic Something" but a supra-individual Cultural-Linguistic-Historical Something. This something does enter into a relation with each individual *Dasein*. It does dominate us. It does send worlds of meaning to us while withholding itself in a realm of mystery, a mystery that is not "preternatural" but historical and thus "preterindividual." This is not, in short, the "reification" of ideas but simply good, honest phenomenology: characterizing the experience of appropriation/the clearing as it actually occurs to us.

There is no question that Heidegger's writing is highly rhetorical, with a penchant for mystical, religious, and prophetic forms of expression. The desire to get through the rhetoric to what Heidegger is really saying is completely understandable and commendable, and Sheehan has done more than any scholar I know to get to Heidegger's real message. But once one arrives at this understanding, one cannot merely give Heidegger's rhetoric the brush-off, like an annoyingly chatty cab driver once he has gotten you to your destination. One has to turn back to the rhetoric and try to understand why Heidegger adopted it in the first place.

One also needs to understand the contents of Heidegger's teachings to separate the purely psychological dimensions of this thought. Heidegger was clearly an odd duck. He writes repeatedly about aberrant mental states in the 1920s and '30s, and in 1945–'46 he suffered a nervous breakdown. Heidegger's biographers can provide many more psychological details. But before a competent psychiatrist tries to make sense of Heidegger's psyche, he should read Sheehan to make sense of his thought.

THE HISTORY OF BEING

Sheehan's chapter 9, "The History of Being" and Conclusion, chapter 10, "Critical Reflections," can be discussed as a unit, because they deal with the same essential subject matter. (Chapter 10 focuses on Heidegger's essay "The Question Concerning Technology," which discusses the *Gestell*, which is the present dispensation in the history of Being.) As usual, Sheehan marshals a host of useful quotations, etymologies, and distinctions.

These chapters deal with Heidegger at his most anti-humanist, anti-modernist, and ultra-conservative. And, as you might already suspect, Sheehan is quite unsympathetic. At one point. Sheehan summarizes what he thinks is of enduring value in Heidegger:

> . . . a phenomenological rereading of traditional being as the meaningfulness of things; a persuasive explanation of how we make sense of things, both in praxis and in apophantic discourse; the grounding of all sense-making

in the *a priori* structure of human being as a mortal dynamism of aheadness-and-return; and, based on all of that, a strong philosophical exhortation, in the tradition of Greek philosophical protreptic, to become what we already are and to live our lives accordingly. (p. 267)

This is basically *Being and Time*, plus a couple of lectures, "What Is Metaphysics?" and "On the Essence of Truth," with a cut-off around the end of 1930.

Heidegger interprets the trajectory of Western—and now global—history as one of decline from classical Greek and Roman civilization to the present day. Heidegger traces this decline in terms of the history of metaphysics, but contra Sheehan, Heidegger does not believe that philosophers are the "hidden legislators" of mankind, i.e., that philosophical ideas are the foundation of culture and the driving force of history. Rather, in keeping with his anti-humanism, Heidegger holds that historical change arises from inscrutable sources, and philosophers, as well as poets like Sophocles and Hölderlin, merely receive and articulate the deepest currents of the *Zeitgeist*.

According to Heidegger, the pre-Socratics and the Attic tragedians articulated the deepest *a priori* assumptions of the classical worldview, namely that mnn is a mortal being inhabiting a splendid world bounded by mystery and necessity, boundaries that man cannot transgress in thought or deed without *hubris* that courts *nemesis*. The deepest *a priori* assumptions of modernity are that all boundaries of thought and action, including human mortality itself, are ultimately temporary, i.e., that everything is in principle knowable and controllable by man.

Heidegger's distinction between the classical and the modern corresponds roughly to Spengler's distinction between classical and Faustian civilizations, although Heidegger places both within a single historical narrative of decline, whereas Spengler regards them as separate civilizational organisms each of which has undergone its own phase of decline, with the decline of the West still occurring today.

Sheehan points out that Heidegger names only two dispensations in the history of Being, both of them modern: the age of the world picture (the *a priori* assumptions of early modernity) and the *Gestell* (the *a priori* assumptions of present-day global technological civilization).

Sheehan dismisses Heidegger's claim that the decline of the West is caused by man's deepening oblivion of the clearing. But setting aside the question of causation, it is actually an accurate description of the decline, for oblivion of the clearing is equivalent to oblivion of human finitude, oblivion of the dependence of the individual on collective embodied meaning, and oblivion of the ineluctable mystery of the ultimate source of meaning—and all of these are traits of the *Gestell*. Forgetting the clearing is forgetting one's place, metaphysically speaking. To the Greeks, this is *hubris*. Technology, surely, can exist without *hubris*. But could modernity?

Sheehan stiches together a wonderful quilt quotation from Heidegger's 1935 lecture course *Introduction to Metaphysics* illustrating Heidegger's conservative lament at the civilizational consequences of modernity:

> . . . the hopeless frenzy of unchained technology and the rootless organization of the average man . . . spiritual decline . . . the darkening of the world, the flight of the gods . . . the destruction of the earth, the reduction of human beings to a mass, the preeminence of the mediocre . . . the disempowering of spirit, its dissolution, diminution, suppression, and misinterpretation . . . all things sinking to the same depths, to a flat surface resembling a dark mirror that no longer reflects anything and gives nothing back . . . the boundless etcetera of the indifferent, the ever-the-same . . . the onslaught of what aggressively destroys all rank, every world-creating impulse of the spirit . . . the regulation and mastery of the material relations of production . . . the instrumentalization and misinterpretation of spirit. (p. 282)

In this same lecture course, Heidegger famously declared that the "inner truth and greatness of National Socialism" was its potential to reverse these tendencies, to preserve human root-edness, distinct identities, and traditional social structures from the deracinating and leveling forces of "global technology." Sheehan suggests that Heidegger added this comment when he edited the lectures for publication in 1953, but if so, it is con-sistent with the rest of the lectures, as indicated by Sheehan's own quilt quotation. (National Socialism falls outside the pur-view of Sheehan's book, but he makes sure we know he's against it.)

Sheehan is also dismissive of Heidegger's postwar thoughts on the way out of the modern dispensation, particularly in his 1949 lecture "The Turn," which is obscure even for Heidegger. The lecture also adds to the confusion about Heidegger's con-cept of the turn by introducing a new sense of *Kehre*. This "turn" refers to the advent of the next dispensation of Being, in which mankind awakens "from oblivion of Being, to oblivion of Being." Here Being refers to the clearing. Oblivion of Being refers to the intrinsic hiddenness of the clearing as well as to our lack of awareness of the intrinsic hiddenness of the clear-ing. Our awakening, therefore, refers to becoming aware of the intrinsic hiddenness of the clearing, which is equivalent to awakening to the fact that we cannot understand and control the dispensations of Being, which should overthrow the hubris-tic assumption that we can understand and control everything.

Sheehan again laments the "perverse rhetoric of hypostati-zation and reification that Heidegger employs, as if Being Itself, after centuries of 'refusing Itself' to humankind, suddenly chooses to turn and show Itself" (p. 265). But again, this is Heidegger's description of how historical change presents itself to him. If the human will cannot control history, but history changes anyway, then history would seem to have a will of its own.

If we cannot control history, then what is the meaning of dissent? If ideas do not shape history, does that imply that dis-senting ideas are merely subjective, private, and ineffectual? Not necessarily. Heidegger would have to hold that dissenting ideas are themselves dispensations of Being. If they are out of step with the present dispensation, perhaps they are the first glimmers of a new one. It is not surprising, therefore, that Heidegger occasionally adopts the tone of a prophet. If you find it annoying, just remember that it is far less pretentious than the idea that philosophers are the architects of history.

Heidegger is just one prophet of this new dispensation. It first stirred in eighteenth-century critics of the Enlightenment like Vico, Rousseau, and Herder. In the nineteenth century, it was taken up by such movements as Romanticism, Transcendentalism, utopian socialism, the pre-Raphaelites, and Arts and Crafts, as well as various Symbolists, Decadents, and dandies. In the twentieth century, it stirred the prophets of deep ecology, agrarianism, and natural living like Aldo Leopold, Savitri Devi, J. R. R. Tolkien, E. F. Schumacher, Wendell Berry, and Carlo Petrini. It overlaps significantly with neo-paganism, Traditionalism, and Western seekers of Eastern wisdom, as well as with mystical and traditional forms of Christianity. It is also at work in the ongoing resistance to globalization, which, according to sociologists Charles Lindholm and José Pedro Zúquete, embraces the European New Right as well as movements of the Left.[9]

We should also remember that the man/meaning relationship is one of mutual dependency. Yes, collective meanings have the advantage in relation to any individual. But meaning depends upon man just as man depends upon meaning. The present dispensation may have claimed and shaped us, but it still needs us to sustain it. That means that each individual faces choices that sustain or undermine the present dispensation.

We sustain it whenever we participate in the global technological system, whenever we demand things that are faster, cheaper, easier, and more available. We undermine it whenever we prefer the local to the global, the beautiful over the useful, the earthy over the plastic, distinct peoples over monoculture and miscegenation, the acceptance of reality over the striving for power, the unique over the mass-produced, the ecosys-

---

[9] Charles Lindholm and José Pedro Zúquete, *The Struggle for the World: Liberation Movements for the Twenty-First Century* (Stanford, Stanford University Press, 2010).

tem over the economic system, etc. Heidegger is just one face in a giant *Sgt. Pepper's* collage of anti-modernists, along with generations of Wandervogel and hippies, historical preservationists and organic gardeners, Identitarians and Zapatistas, monkeywrenchers and tree-spikers, druids and swamis, down to flannel-clad hipsters tending bees and brewing beer in Brooklyn. When enough of us live *as if* the new dispensation is already here, perhaps it will arrive.

Sheehan complains that Heidegger's account of the *a priori* assumptions of modernity is not based on fine-grained historical analysis. I guess it seems insufficiently inductive to him. (Yes, the oil industry seems in the grip of world-dominating hubris. But what about the coal industry?) But this seems to miss the point. We will not encounter the *a priori* assumptions of modernity in front of us, for they are already behind us, *within us*, structuring how we see the world and ourselves. Since we are all more or less modern men, we can test the truth of Heidegger's claims simply through self-reflection.

Sheehan dates himself a bit by complaining that the 96 volumes of Heidegger's *Complete Edition* published to date make no mention of *Kapitalismus*—as if Heidegger's analysis of modernity needed recourse to Marxist buzzwords, as if he had not transcended the opposition of capitalism and socialism and revealed their underlying metaphysical identity.

Although I am nonplussed by Sheehan's criticisms of Heidegger, I have some of my own. I am skeptical of his post-Kantian transcendental quarantine of metaphysics, and I am not so sure that the clearing is intrinsically hidden at all, or hidden in a non-trivial way.

But my main objection to Heidegger is his terrible writing. I long ago lost count of the Heideggerian words that actually don't mean what they seem to mean. Heidegger translator David Farrell Krell recounts:

Occasionally, I would bring [Heidegger] a text of his that simply would not reveal his meaning; he would read it over several times, grimace, shake his head slightly, and say, "Das ist aber schlecht!" (That is really bad!).[10]

I wish I could get back every hour I wasted reading Derrida and Foucault. I don't feel the same way about Heidegger. But especially with certain works, I feel like those South African miners who have to sift through mountains of rubble for a pocketful of gems. When it comes to making sense of Heidegger, the philosopher was his own worst enemy, which makes Thomas Sheehan's scholarly career a work of friendship. *Making Sense of Heidegger* is an indispensable book on an unavoidable thinker.[11]

Counter-Currents, December 12, 2014

---

[10] David Farrell Krell, "Work Sessions with Martin Heidegger," *Philosophy Today* 26 (1982), p. 138.

[11] As a book, *Making Sense of Heidegger* is not particularly attractive, but it is well-edited. I spotted only a few mistakes: p. ix, GA 6 should be *Nietzsche*, vols. 1 and 2; p. 210: "breaks" should be "brakes"; p. 262: "synchronic" and "diachronic" are reversed.

THE GODS OF THE FOREST

This is what I believe:
"That I am I."
"That my soul is a dark forest."
"That my known self will never be more than a little clearing in the forest."
"That gods, strange gods, come forth from the forest into the clearing of my known self, and then go back."
"That I must have the courage to let them come and go."

— D. H. Lawrence[1]

The "clearing" (*Lichtung*) is one of Heidegger's most vivid but elusive ideas. The *Lichtung* appears throughout Heidegger's career, from his first book, *Being and Time* (1927) to his late lectures and seminars, especially "The End of Philosophy and the Task of Thinking" (1963–64).

This is the first appearance of the clearing in *Being and Time*:

When we talk in an ontically figurative way about the *lumen naturale* in human being, we mean nothing other than the existential-ontological structure of this being, the fact that it *is* in such a way as to be its there [*Da*]. To say that it is "illuminated" [*erleuchtet*] means that it is cleared [*gelichtet*] in itself *as* being-in-the-world, not by another being, but in such a way that it *is* itself the clearing [*Lichtung*]. Only for a being thus cleared [*gelichteten*] existentially do present-at-hand-beings [*Vorhandenes*] become accessible in the light or concealed in the darkness.[2]

---

[1] D. H. Lawrence, "Benjamin Franklin," in *Studies in Classic American Literature* (New York: Thomas Seltzer, 1923).

[2] Martin Heidegger, *Being and Time*, trans. Joan Stambaugh and Dennis J. Schmidt (Albany: SUNY Press, 2010), p. 129; *Sein und Zeit* (Tübingen: Niemeyer, 1986), p. 133.

Heidegger's language is intimidating, but his meaning is clear. "*Lumen naturale*" is Latin for "light of nature." In medieval scholastic philosophy, it refers to the natural powers of mankind to know reality. The light of nature streams out from the human being and renders the world intelligible. It is the object-directed beam of consciousness, the subject-object relationship. Heidegger claims that the *lumen naturale* is a figurative way of talking about the human being as knower.

Heidegger uses the word "*Dasein*" to refer to human beings as knowers. *Dasein* is a German word for existence, but Heidegger hears it as a compound of "*Da*" and "*Sein*." *Da* means here/there, i.e., place, and *Sein* means "Being." *Dasein* is thus *the place where Being happens*. Hence Heidegger's claim that the human knower "*is* in such a way as to be its there [*Da*]."

For Heidegger "Being" means *the presence and absence of beings to Dasein*. Hence his talk about *Dasein* as the being for whom "present-at-hand-beings [*Vorhandenes*] become accessible in the light [present] or concealed in the darkness [absent]."

How is the "light of nature" connected to "the place where Being happens" (*Dasein*)? The connection Heidegger draws is a metaphor that is also *almost* a play on words: "To say that it [the *Da* or "place" in *Dasein*] is 'illuminated' [*erleuchtet*] means that it is cleared [*gelichtet*] in itself *as* being-in-the-world, not by another being, but in such a way that it *is* itself the clearing [*Lichtung*]."

The German word *Lichtung* means "clearing," as in a forest clearing, a kind of place (*Da*), but it also contains "*Licht*," the German word for light. Thus the *Lichtung* seems like the perfect way of connecting the *lumen naturale* to a place where knowledge happens.

What is the link between *Lichtung* and *Licht*? It seems like a straightforward etymological connection, but it is not that simple. First of all, the sense of *Lichtung* as a forest clearing is not derived from *Licht* but from the verb *lichten*, which does not mean to lighten in the sense of "to illuminate" but to lighten in the sense of "to free" or "to unburden," as in clearing away trees and brush to create a free and open space. In the passage above, Heidegger is clearly aware that *Lichtung* is derived from *lichten*, hence he says that being *erleuchtet* (illuminated) presupposes being *gelichtet* (cleared).

Second, there seems to be a straightforward *material* connection between the *Lichtung* and *Licht*, for the *Lichtung* allows light to penetrate to the forest floor and illuminate it. But again, it is not so simple. The *Lichtung* as clearing is not merely a space for light/presence but also for the dark (*das Dunkel*)/absence. In its primary sense, a *Lichtung* is a free and open space, a place where one can encounter things both in the light and in the dark.

Perhaps to correct misunderstandings of the *Lichtung* in *Being and Time*, Heidegger revisited the concept in his later writings, such as "The End of Philosophy and the Task of Thinking":

> The forest *Lichtung* is experienced in contrast to dense forest, called *Dickung* in our older language. The substantive *Lichtung* goes back to the verb *lichten*. . . . To lighten something means to make it light, free, and open, e.g., to make the forest free of trees at once place. The free space thus originating is the *Lichtung*. . . . Light can stream into the clearing, into its openness, and let brightness play with darkness in it. But light never first creates the *Lichtung*. Rather, light presupposes it. The clearing is the open region for everything that becomes present and absent.[3]

Heidegger's concept of the *Lichtung* does not fundamentally change with the development of his philosophy. What changes are (1) the context in which he discusses it and (2) his evaluation of its importance. In *Being and Time*, the *Lichtung* is discussed in passing in the context of what Heidegger called "transcendental-horizonal thinking." In Heidegger's later work, the *Lichtung* becomes a central concept in the context of what he called "Being-historical thinking." (We will define these terms presently.)

The horizon is one of the most commonly used concepts in continental philosophy. The horizon is the edge of our world.

The most common sense of horizon is "as far as the eye can

---

[3] "The End of Philosophy and the Task of Thinking," trans. Joan Stambaugh, in Martin Heidegger, *Basic Writings*, ed. David Farrell Krell (London: Routledge, 2011), p. 319.

see." If you are on a "flat" surface, like the prairies of Saskatchewan or the surface of the ocean, you feel like you can see to the middle of next week. How far you can see depends on your height, of course, but on a "flat" surface, we can see a few miles to the horizon, where the earth's curvature drops away, hiding what lies beyond it.

On the surface of the earth, the horizon is a circle. When we look above us, at the sky, by day it seems infinite, but at night, when stars and planets become visible, it is natural to envision the horizon as a star-studded hemisphere, the celestial dome. And if we are suspended in space, it is natural to envision the horizon as a sphere.

Hold fast to this image of a sphere. There was a time when consciousness did not exist. Beings existed, of course. Even living beings existed, like plants and primitive animals. But they were without consciousness, or with only the most primitive forms of consciousness, such as touch and taste. Such beings may have jostled and groped one another, even consumed and savored one another. But they did not *know* one other, meaning: they did not encounter one another at a distance, in a space. Thus one can envision the emergence of consciousness as a bubble—a spherical horizon in which objects can be encountered at a distance—opening in the midst of the density and darkness of blind nature.

The second sense of horizon is "the edge of the visual field." Fix your eyes on a point in the distance. Place your hands in front of that point. Then move them to the left and the right, keeping your eyes fixed on the same spot. At a certain point, your hands will pass beyond a fuzzy line and disappear from your field of vision. That fuzzy line is its horizon.

Both senses of horizon are *human-centered* concepts. Horizons are *relative* to the observer.

The first kind of horizon is as far as *your* eyes can see. The horizon is not fixed. It moves with you. It expands as you rise above the surface of the earth, and when you enter outer space, it extends untold billions of miles to the farthest visible object.

The second kind of horizon is the edge of *your* visual field. When you turn your head, the horizon turns with you. Things that were previously invisible become visible, and things that were previously visible slip beyond the horizon and disappear.

Both senses of horizon are primarily defined in terms of vision: as far as the *eye* can see, the edge of the *visual* field. But there are more ways of knowing than just seeing. There is an auditory horizon as well: a distance beyond which we cannot hear things. There are also olfactory horizons: things too far away to smell.

There are also auditory and olfactory equivalents of the edge of our visual field, horizons that shift as we move our ears and noses. Taste and touch, however, do not take place at a distance at all. They require contact, so they do not have the equivalent of the first kind of horizon, but they do have the equivalent of the second kind of horizon, namely the moving edge of our hands or tongues as we explore the objects they touch.

There is more to knowledge than just the senses. Concepts name individuals as well as whole kinds. Scientific and philosophical theories, as well as literary and religious narratives, extend our knowledge far beyond the visible.

We can also distinguish a third sense of horizon: the *transcendental* horizon. Knowledge only happens under certain conditions. These conditions can be divided into subjective and objective.

The objective conditions of knowledge are the things that are known. If there is no object, there is no knowledge. The object is "transcendent," meaning that it "transcends" consciousness by being beyond it.

The "transcendental" is not the object. It refers to the *subjective* conditions of knowledge, i.e., what we contribute to knowing. We contribute both hardware and software to consciousness, the hardware being the universal and necessary structures and activities of our sense organs and brains, the software being our particular and contingent languages and experiences.[4]

---

[4] Software is not a perfect analogy, because we create software for computers, but we do not create the software of our own consciousness in the same way. Because we create software, we fully understand and control it. But language and culture evolved along with

For simplicity's sake, let's focus on the visible. The things that show up within the boundaries of your visual field (Horizon 2), as far as the eye can see (Horizon 1), are the objects of consciousness. These objects appear to us by virtue of our sense organs. They *make sense* to us in terms of our memories: our individual experiences and the collective experience of mankind present in our language and culture. When you see a green lawn, a bed of flowers, and an unwelcome piece of litter, you encounter them as meaningful in terms of your personal experience, language, and cultural expectations.

It is tempting to think of the hardware and software of consciousness as operating just behind the horizon of our visual field, i.e., outside the field of our awareness. They lurk in the dark woods, outside the clearing. When we see things, we do not see our eyes. We *look through* our eyes at visible objects. When we name and interpret these objects, we do not think about words. We use words to *think about* the objects. First and foremost, we are conscious of things, not conscious of our own consciousness. We are conscious of the transcendent, not the transcendental.

But we have the power to *turn our attention toward* consciousness. This kind of "reflection" is one of the tasks of philosophy. Although we are primarily engaged with *objects present in the world*, we can shift our focus and reflect on *how objects become present to us*. This form of philosophy is known as *phenomenology*.

Almost from the start, philosophers have reflected on the conditions for the possibility of knowledge. This reflective turn intensified with early modern philosophy. But early modern philosophers interpreted the transcendental conditions of knowledge as objects *within* the realm of consciousness, objects that *fill up* the horizon of consciousness, which led to the question: If we are aware of objects *inside* our consciousness, what relationship—if any—do the inner objects of consciousness have to an *external* world? The transcendental approach to philosophy, beginning with Kant and culminating with Husserl's phe-

---

human beings. We did not create them, do not fully understand them, and cannot fully control them.

nomenology, avoids this skeptical trap.[5]

In *Being and Time*, the *Lichtung* is identified with *Dasein*, the human being *qua* knower. *Lichtung/Dasein* is a space in which things can appear, which is to say that *Lichtung/Dasein* is the transcendental horizon. This makes sense, as Heidegger began his career as a transcendental phenomenologist. He was Husserl's star student and heir apparent.

I believe that Heidegger remained a transcendental phenomenologist throughout his career, insofar as he always maintained that the presence of beings has both transcendental and transcendent conditions. There needs to be an object, and we need to be capable of experiencing it. If there is no object, then nothing shows up. If we are not capable of experiencing an object, then nothing shows up. If there is an object, and we are able to experience it, knowledge happens.

But Heidegger increasingly obscured the transcendental-phenomenological nature of his thinking because he wished to distance himself from three common misunderstandings of this approach.

First, how things become present to us is not merely a matter of the universal and necessary "hardware" of consciousness. It is also a matter of historically contingent and variable "software" such as languages and cultures.

Second, we should never confuse phenomenology with the bad forms of modern philosophy that lose track of the external world by denigrating our ability to know anything outside of our consciousness.

Third, phenomenology is not a form of modern "humanism":

---

[5] Kant accepted that human consciousness is finite, meaning that we can only know objects insofar as they can appear to our particular form of consciousness, i.e., insofar as they can enter our transcendental horizon. But what appears in our transcendental horizon is not a realm of inner representations, crowding out our view of the external world. It *is* the external world, insofar as it can be given to us.

Husserl clarified the relationship between ordinary consciousness and philosophical reflection so that the transcendental conditions of knowledge can no longer be confused with an inner world of representations blocking our access to the world of objects.

the grandiose delusion that nothing can resist our drive for ever greater knowledge and power.

To shake off these misunderstandings, Heidegger recast phenomenology in a radically new vocabulary—which invited a whole host of new misunderstandings.

For example, whereas Kant claimed that every object of knowledge has two aspects: the *phenomenal*, which is the object insofar as it is given to the human knower, and the *noumenal*, which is the object insofar as it transcends our awareness. In "The Origin of the Work of Art," Heidegger speaks of the same two aspects as "world" and "earth."[6] A being is known to us insofar as it enters into "world," meaning the transcendental horizon. The aspect of a being that transcends our awareness of it is its "earthy" dimension. This is classic transcendental philosophy recast in poetic language reminiscent of the pre-Socratic philosophers or Friedrich Hölderlin.

In *Being and Time*, Heidegger's focus is on how the temporal structure of human consciousness is the horizon in which present objects become meaningful. It is a *tour-de-force* of transcendental phenomenology. But Heidegger believed that a transcendental account of meaning in terms of universal structures and activities of consciousness was inadequate. Heidegger did not regard *Dasein* as a "transcendental ego," common to all men, a cosmopolitan "view from nowhere." Instead, *Dasein* is a view from somewhere: a particular culturally and historically conditioned outlook.

Thus Heidegger's later philosophy focuses on how the individual mind is embedded in collective, evolved historical practices—i.e., cultures and languages—that are always plural. These practices are ways of making sense of things. These sense-giving practices are what I have called the "software" of consciousness.

---

[6] There are two English translations of "The Origin of the Work of Art": Albert Hofstadter's is in *Poetry, Language, Thought*, ed. and trans. by Albert Hofstadter (New York: Harper & Row, 1971) as well as the *Basic Writings* collection; Julian Young's is in *Off the Beaten Track*, ed. and trans. by Julian Young and Kenneth Haynes (Cambridge: Cambridge University Press, 2002).

To be economical with words, I am simply going to refer to *sense-making practices* and *practical knowledge*, with the understanding that these take many different forms.

Heidegger calls his later approach to philosophy "Being-historical thinking." "Being" refers to how beings become present, and the "historical" refers to the evolved, contingent, and mutable bodies of practical knowledge that form the horizon in which beings become present.

Heidegger believed that all human sense-making takes place within the historical clearing, but his primary focus is philosophy. Hence in "The End of Philosophy and the Task of Thinking," he discusses the clearing as what is "unthought" in the philosophical tradition, using Hegel and Husserl as examples:

> . . . what remains unthought in the matter of philosophy as well as its method? Speculative dialectic [in the Hegelian sense] is a mode in which the matter of philosophy comes to appear of itself and for itself, and thus becomes present [*Gegenwart*]. Such appearance necessarily occurs in luminosity. Only by virtue of some sort of brightness can what shines show itself, that is, radiate. But brightness in its turn rests upon something open, something free, which it might illuminate here and there, now and then. Brightness plays in the open and strives there with darkness. Wherever a present being encounters another present being or even only lingers near it . . . there openness already rules, the free region is in play. Only this openness grants to the movement of speculative thinking the passage through what it thinks.
>
> We call this openness that grants a possible letting appear and show "clearing." (pp. 318–19)

For Heidegger, the subject matter (*Sache*) of philosophy is the "Being of beings," which is equivalent to "the presence of what is present" (p. 320). For Heidegger, however, beings become present through the interplay of presence *and* absence. The clearing is the space in which beings are encountered in their presence and absence: "Whether or not what is present is experienced, comprehended, or presented, presence as lingering in the open always remains dependent upon the prevalent clearing. What is absent too, cannot be as such unless it presences in the *free space of the clearing*" (p. 320).

The clearing is the context in which beings become present to us. It also names the context in which the Being of beings becomes present to philosophical reflection. It might be best, however, to speak of these as different clearings, because they are correlated to different forms of consciousness, i.e., ordinary consciousness and philosophical reflection.

Heidegger claims that even though the clearing allows things to become present, it itself remains absent:

> All philosophical thinking that explicitly or inexplicitly follows the call "to the matter itself" is in its movement and with its method already admitted to the free space of the clearing. But philosophy knows nothing of the clearing. Philosophy does speak about the light of reason, but does not heed the clearing of Being. The *lumen naturale*, the light of reason, throws light only on the open. It does concern the clearing, but so little does it form it that it needs it in order to be able to illuminate what is present in the clearing. (p. 320)

But although Heidegger claims that philosophy knows nothing of the clearing, he does suggest that at the beginning of the Western philosophical tradition Parmenides *unknowingly* spoke about the clearing as "the untrembling heart of unconcealment [*aletheia*], well-rounded." *Aletheia* (ἀλήθεια) is usually translated as "truth," but Heidegger hears it as a combination of *lethe* (λήθη, concealment, oblivion) and the privative prefix ἀ, meaning "un," hence unconcealment.

To describe unconcealment as "well-rounded" brings to mind the spherical horizon, the bubble of consciousness that allows humans to encounter objects within its context. It is the clearing, the transcendental horizon.

Having equated the clearing with *aletheia* as unconcealment, Heidegger returns to the question of why philosophy does not know the clearing/unconcealment:

> How is it that *aletheia*, unconcealment, appears to man's
> natural experience and speech only as correctness and de-
> pendability? Is it because man's ecstatic sojourn in the
> openness of presencing is turned only toward what is pre-
> sent and the presentation of what is present? [Heidegger's
> answer to this question is "yes."] But what else does this
> mean than that presence as such, and together with it the
> clearing that grants it, remains unheeded? Only what
> *aletheia* as clearing grants is experienced and thought, not
> what it is as such. This remains concealed.

Heidegger's point is that the clearing/unconcealment is hidden to philosophy because philosophy is focused on what appears *in* the clearing, not upon the clearing itself. This pattern
can be observed in all forms of consciousness: our senses perceive objects, not themselves; when we use language to talk
about things, we are not paying attention to language. As a general rule: when we are conscious of objects, we are not conscious
of the conditions that make consciousness possible. Our focus
cannot be two places at once. So if we are focused on what appears in the clearing, we are not aware of the clearing itself.

The concealment of the clearing is not, therefore, a matter of
chance or momentary inattention. It is a *necessary* feature of consciousness. But Heidegger does not wish to speak about it in
terms of consciousness and its acts. Instead, in keeping with the
anti-humanism of his later philosophy, he ascribes "agency" to
the clearing itself:

> Does [the concealment of the clearing] happen by chance?
> [Heidegger's answer is no.] Does it happen only as a con-
> sequence of the carelessness of human thinking? [No
> again.] Or does it happen because self-concealing, con-
> cealment, *lethe*, belongs to *a-letheia*, not as shadow to light,
> but rather as the heart of *aletheia*? [Yes.] Moreover, does
> not a sheltering and preserving rule in this self-concealing
> of the clearing of presence, from which alone unconceal-

ment can be granted, so that which is present can appear in its presence? [Again, yes.]

If this were so, then the clearing would not be the mere clearing of presence, but the clearing of presence conceal-ing itself, the clearing of a self-concealing sheltering. (pp. 323–24)

In other late texts, Heidegger calls the self-concealing of the clearing the "oblivion of Being." In the world of technological nihilism—which Heidegger describes as the completion of the metaphysical tradition—not only are we oblivious of the clear-ing that makes presence possible, we are perfectly complacent about this fact. We are oblivious of our own oblivion.

How does the concept of the clearing undermine modern humanism? Heidegger claims that all knowledge, not just phi-losophy, depends upon the clearing. The clearing, however, con-sists of evolved, historically contingent sense-making practices. These practices are learned primarily by imitation, beginning in early childhood, far before the dawn of self-consciousness, much less critical reason.

To the modern humanist, these practices are "prejudices" that are accepted on mere authority and lack any rational foundation. Thus they are unworthy guides to life. To give these prejudices a rational foundation, we must be able to put them into words, specifically into *propositions* that can be verified or falsified. These propositions must then be tested for truth. The true ones will be kept, the false ones discarded.

This project presupposes that the sovereign intellect can fully know itself and cut all ties to beliefs that it cannot rationally jus-tify. Moreover, the purgation of prejudice and reconstruction of the self is merely a prelude to the conquest and reconstruction of nature as a whole.

Heidegger's critique of this sort of humanism is fundamental.

First, the self cannot fully know itself. Every act of conscious-ness focuses on its object, not itself. This is true even of self-consciousness. When we reflect on ourselves, we split con-sciousness into an object that is reflected upon and an act of re-flection, which is focused on its object, not itself. No matter how many times we might try to turn consciousness on itself (reflecting upon reflecting upon reflecting upon consciousness), this pattern persists. No act of consciousness is conscious of itself. Consciousness forgets itself in order to focus on its object, even when that object is another part of the same consciousness.

Second, the whole process of reflecting upon, articulating, and testing sense-making practices requires the use of these practices. For instance, we cannot criticize language without using language. There is no Archimedean point from which one can survey, test, and reconstruct the whole of one's practical knowledge. Thus such a critical process can only be partial and presupposes a background horizon of practices that we simply *use* rather than reflect upon and criticize, i.e., the very sort of "prejudices" that we are supposed to reject.

Third, there are limits to our ability to articulate and test knowledge. Perceptual and practical knowledge, in particular, cannot be fully articulated into words and tested. In these spheres, *we always know more than we can say.* Articulate propositional knowledge like "I own a big, blue bicycle" can be verified or falsified. But your ability to *ride* your bicycle, or your sense as a native speaker that "blue, big bicycle" is wrong and "big, blue bicycle" is right, cannot be articulated and tested in the same way. You can test your ability to ride a bicycle, or to speak about it, only by actually *doing* so. By demanding we discard all knowledge that does not meet the narrow model of articulate, propositional knowledge, modern humanism amounts to the imperative to make ourselves stupid.

Thus Heidegger agrees with our epigraph from D. H. Lawrence: "my soul is a dark forest. . . . my known self will never be more than a little clearing in the forest." The modern humanist thinks the forest is full of monsters only because he believes that the darkness destroys the clearing rather than makes it possible. Heidegger, however, sees the forest as filled with beneficent powers: the traditions of practical knowledge that connect us to our ancestors, grant us a collective destiny, and open up the clearing before us. Thus, like Lawrence, he can say that "gods, strange gods, come forth from the forest into the clearing of my known self, and then go back." Not everything handed down to us is good, of course, so there is no guarantee that we won't be swept up in a wild hunt from time to time. But we cannot fundamentally understand, control, or reconstruct these traditions, and if we try, we will be cut off from their illuminating and life-giving power. Thus we need to relinquish the mania for control and have the courage to let the gods of the forest come and go.

Counter-Currents, August 10, 2020

NIETZSCHE, METAPHYSICS, & NIHILISM*

One of Heidegger's most striking claims is that modern nihilism is the consummation of Western metaphysics. Generally, people think of nihilism and metaphysics as polar opposites. Nihilism is associated with the dissolution of an objective world into subjective impressions, the transformation of objective values into subjective preferences, the loss of shared meanings and a common frame of reference. Traditionally, metaphysics upholds the objectivity of reality, knowledge, and values. But Heidegger argues that the metaphysics of objectivity actually leads to nihilism in the end.

To understand this argument, I wish to comment on one of my favorite texts by Heidegger, a pair of lectures entitled "The Eternal Recurrence of the Same and the Will to Power." These lectures beautifully epitomize Heidegger's vast two-volume work on Nietzsche, and they gather together and display the unity of themes discussed by Heidegger over a period of more than fifty years.

Heidegger's thesis is that "Nietzsche's philosophy is the consummation of Western metaphysics."[1] For Heidegger, Nietzsche's philosophy represents the epitome of modern nihilism, the ultimate manifestation of the nihilistic impulse built into Western metaphysics from the very beginning. Heidegger's claim that Nietzsche is the last metaphysician of the West is a stunning thesis, a thesis very difficult to defend, for Nietzsche is widely regarded as the first post-metaphysical thinker, not the last metaphysical thinker.

Traditional metaphysics is constructed around the dualisms

---

* From an adult education class on "Heidegger, Metaphysics, & Nihilism" given in Atlanta in the mid-1990s.

[1] Martin Heidegger, *Nietzsche*, vol. III: *The Will to Power as Knowledge and as Metaphysics*, ed. David Farrell Krell, trans. Joan Stambaugh, David Farrell Krell, and Frank A. Capuzzi (New York: Harper & Row, 1987), p. 161.

of *permanence* and *change* and of *appearance* and *reality*. The permanent is identified with Being, which is said to be a reality that lies beyond the world of appearances, the world of change, the realm of becoming. Nietzsche seems to overcome these dualisms by collapsing the distinctions between permanence and change, appearance and reality, Being and becoming. Therefore, Nietzsche seems to go beyond metaphysics.

How, then, does Heidegger establish that Nietzsche was the last metaphysician of the West? Another way of putting this question is: How does Heidegger establish that Nietzsche's attempt to overcome metaphysics is a failure? What does Heidegger think that a genuine overcoming of metaphysics requires?

NIETZSCHE'S METAPHYSICS

When Heidegger uses the word "metaphysics" pejoratively, he refers to the metaphysics of *presence*: "These positions take the Being of beings as having been determined in the sense of permanence of presence."[2] Another word for the metaphysics of presence in the Heidegger lexicon is "Platonism." Platonism cannot necessarily be identified with Plato's own views. Platonism, rather, is the pervasive *interpretation* of Plato's views in the tradition.

Platonism identifies Being with *permanence* as opposed to change, *presence* as opposed to absence, *identity* as opposed to difference. The latter terms of these pairs—change, absence, difference—are identified with non-being.

In the world around us, rest and motion, presence and absence, identity and difference are all mixed together. Thus the Platonist concludes that this world is not the true world; it is not the realm of Being, but the realm of *becoming*, which is a mere blurred image or decayed manifestation of Being.

Becoming is merely a veil of appearances that cloaks and hides that which is real, namely Being.

The Platonic realm of Being is identified as the place of forms or essences. The world of becoming is where we find in-

---

[2] Heidegger, *Nietzsche*, vol. III, p. 162.

dividual men, individual dogs, individual chairs, individual tables. All of these individuals come into being, change, and pass out of existence. The world of Being contains not individual men, but the *essence* of man, or "manhood." It does not contain individual dogs, but the essence of dog, "doghood."

Forms or essences, unlike individuals, do not come into being; they do not change; and they do not pass away. While particulars exist in time, forms of essences exist outside of time, in eternity.

Because particulars in time are infected with change, absence, and difference, we cannot have *certain knowledge* of them; at best, we can have only *tentative opinions* about things in the world around us. We can have certain knowledge only of the unchanging forms or essences in the realm of Being.

Heidegger holds that the metaphysics of presence—the interpretation of Being as presence—and also the Platonic distinction between the world of Being and the world of becoming is retained in Nietzsche's allegedly post-metaphysical doctrines of the *Will to Power* and the *Eternal Recurrence of the Same.*

Nietzsche called the ultimate constituent of the world Will to Power. This is a highly anthropomorphized name for something that is neither a will (for there is no agent behind it that wills); nor is it "to power" (for it is not directed toward the goal of power, or any other goal). Will to Power is Nietzsche's name for *chaos.* Heidegger defines the "Will to Power" as "the essence of power itself. It consists in power's overpowering, that is, its self-enhancement to the highest possible degree."[3]

The Will to Power is the constant exercise of power as an end in itself.

The Will to Power makes possible the constant exercise of power by positing limits for itself and then exceeding them; Will to Power first freezes itself into particular forms and then overcomes and dissolves them.

The Will to Power is Nietzsche's account of what the world is.

The Eternal Recurrence of the Same is a concept derived

---

[3] Heidegger, *Nietzsche*, vol. III, p. 163.

from the ancient Epicureans and Stoics. Both the Stoics and Epicureans believed that the cosmos is finite. The cosmos consists
of matter and void, and there is only so much matter and so
much void. Matter, however, is not fully inert. Matter has both
inert and non-inert dimensions. Matter has the tendency to remain at rest or in motion, which the Epicureans represented by
matter falling through the void. But matter also has a non-inert
aspect that causes it to swerve from its fall or to move from rest
to motion by its own power. The Epicureans represented this
aspect of matter as the famous "*clinamen*" or "swerve" of the
atoms. The Stoics represented this as divine logos, which, following Heraclitus, they represented as fire. Matter, in short, is
in some sense *vital* and *animate*; it is alive and ensouled. Matter's vital principle allows order to form out of chaos. Matter's
inert dimension allows order to dissolve back into chaos.

Given a finite amount of matter and a finite void, the tendency of matter to both create and destroy order, and infinite
time, the Epicureans and Stoics were forced to conclude that
the random play of matter over infinite time not only gives rise
to order, but gives rise to the *same* order *an infinite number of
times*. Everything that is happening now has already happened
an infinite number of times before and will happen an infinite
number of times in the future. The Same will Recur Eternally,
hence the Eternal Recurrence of the Same.

Woody Allen one remarked about the Eternal Recurrence of
the Same, "Great. That means I'll have to sit through the Ice
Capades again."[4] Even worse, he has *already* sat through it an
infinite number of times. It's *deja-vu* all over again.

Nietzsche's Will to Power corresponds precisely to the two
aspects of matter discussed by the Epicureans and Stoics. The
animate aspect of matter that gives rise to form and organization corresponds to the Will to Power's tendency to posit order.
The inert aspect of matter that causes form and organization to
dissolve back into chaos corresponds to the Will to Power's
tendency to overpower and dissolve the very order that it posits.

---

[4] Woody Allen, *Hannah and Her Sisters* (1986).

Nietzsche holds that the Will to Power is finite and that time is infinite. Endlessly rearranging a finite Will to Power over an infinite amount of time means that the same kinds of order will inevitably repeat themselves, and they will repeat themselves an infinite number of times: Eternal Recurrence of the Same.

Just as Will to Power is Nietzsche's account of *what* the world is, the Eternal Recurrence of the Same is Nietzsche's account of *how* the world is.

Nietzsche claims to have abolished metaphysics because he abolishes the dualisms of appearance and reality, Being and becoming, presence and absence, identity and difference, etc. All of these pairs of opposites are found blended together in the Will to Power and the Eternal Recurrence of the Same. There is no realm of pure presence, pristine identity, total rest, and separate essences, lying behind the world that appears to us.

Heidegger's critique of this claim is twofold. First, he argues that the basic elements of Platonism are still at work in Nietzsche. Second, he argues that Nietzsche really does not understand what it would take to overcome metaphysics.

HOW IS NIETZSCHE A METAPHYSICIAN?

Heidegger argues that Nietzsche's doctrines of Eternal Recurrence and Will to Power are metaphysical in two ways. First, the accounts of Eternal Recurrence and Will to Power still buy into the metaphysics of presence. As Heidegger puts it:

> "Recurrence" thinks the permanentizing of what becomes, thinks it to the point where the becoming of what becomes is secured in the duration of its becoming. The "eternal" links the permanentizing of such constancy in the direction of its circling back into itself and forward toward itself. What becomes is not the unceasing otherness of an endlessly changing manifold. What becomes is the same itself, and that means the one and selfsame (the identical) that in each case is within the difference of the other. . . . Nietzsche's thought thinks the constant permanentizing of the becoming of whatever becomes into the

only kind of presence there is — the self-recapitulation of the identical.[5]

Elsewhere, Heidegger writes:

> Will to Power may now be conceived of as the permanentizing of surpassment, that is of becoming; hence as a transformed determination of the guiding metaphysical projection. The Eternal Recurrence of the Same unfurls and displays its essence, so to speak, as the most constant permanentizing of the becoming of what is constant.[6]

Will to Power and the Eternal Recurrence of the Same, in short, think Being in terms of presence too, by making becoming itself permanent, by making becoming recapitulate the identical, by making the motion of becoming circular, thus bringing a kind of eternity into time itself.

Heidegger's second argument for why Nietzsche is a metaphysician is somewhat strained:

> From the outset, the Eternal Recurrence of the Same and Will to Power are grasped as fundamental determinations of beings as such and as a whole — Will to Power as the peculiar coinage of "what-being" . . . and Eternal Recurrence of the Same as the coinage of "that-being."[7]

Heidegger claims that this distinction is "co-extensive" with the basic distinction that defines and sustains metaphysics. "What-being" or "whatness" refers to the *identity* of beings. "That-being" or "thatness" refers to the *existence* of beings. To talk about the identity of a thing is to talk about *what* it is — as opposed to different things. When we talk about the existence of something, we are talking about the fact *that* it is — as opposed to its non-existence.

---

[5] Heidegger, *Nietzsche*, vol. III, pp. 164–65.
[6] Heidegger, *Nietzsche*, vol. III, p. 167.
[7] Heidegger, *Nietzsche*, vol. III, p. 168.

Now, in Platonism, the identity of a particular being is endowed by its form. A particular dog has its identity as a dog because it is related to the Form of dog, or "dogness." A particular man has his identity as a man because he is related somehow to the essence of man, or "manhood." A particular dog has his existence as a concrete individual dog because a bit of the material world has been "informed" by the essence of dog. So, for Platonism, the *identity* or *whatness* of a particular being is explained by its *essence*, and its individual *existence* or *thatness* is explained by its *materiality*.

Heidegger holds that this Platonic distinction is present in the distinction between the Will to Power and the Eternal Recurrence of the Same. Will to Power names the whatness or identity of all beings. Therefore, it corresponds to the Platonic form. Eternal Recurrence names the thatness or existence of beings. Therefore, it corresponds to the instantiation of the Platonic Form in the spatio-temporal-material world. Will to Power is the principle of identity. Eternal Recurrence is the principle of existence. This dualism, Heidegger claims, is not overcome by Nietzsche, so Nietzsche does not overcome metaphysics. (But can we really get "beyond" the distinction between existence and identity?)

Indeed, Heidegger claims that Nietzsche represents the *culmination* of metaphysics. To understand this, we must understand how, precisely, Nietzsche fails to *overcome* metaphysics. And to understand this, we need to know what Heidegger thinks a *genuine* overcoming of metaphysics would require. This requires that we delve into Heidegger's most distinctive and inscrutable topic: "the history of Being." Heidegger's "history of Being" refers specifically to the history of *interpretations* of Being, i.e., the history of metaphysics.

WHAT CONSTITUTES A TRUE OVERCOMING OF METAPHYSICS?

Heidegger mentions the history of Being in a number of places in these two lectures:

What this unleashing of power to its essence is [i.e., that which gives rise to the interpretation of Being as Will to

Power], Nietzsche is unable to think. Nor can any metaphysics think it, inasmuch as metaphysics cannot put the
matter [*die Sache*, the topic] into question.[8]

Metaphysics thinks about Being. But the mind cannot be in two
places at the same time. Thus, if metaphysics *thinks about Being*,
it cannot also reflect upon *what makes thinking about Being possible*. Metaphysics does not think about *the conditions that make
possible its various interpretations of Being*. This is Heidegger's
topic. Therefore, Heidegger's thinking occupies a place *beyond*
metaphysics. Ontology is the branch of metaphysics that deals
with Being. Heidegger claims, however, to be doing "fundamental ontology," which deals with what makes ontology possible. Heidegger gives a number of names to the topic of fundamental ontology. Instead of talking about Being, fundamental ontology deals with the sense or meaning (*Sinn*) of Being,
the truth (*Wahrheit*) of Being, and the clearing (*Lichtung*) of Being.

For Heidegger, interpretations of Being have a history, and
this history has a specific character:

This "selfsame" [Being interpreted as Eternal Recurrence]
is separated as by an abyss from the singularity of the
unrepeatable enjoining of all that coheres. Out of that enjoining alone does the difference commence.[9]

Here Heidegger contrasts Nietzsche's Eternal Recurrence of the
Same with his own view of the history of Being as *a sequence of
unrepeatable contingent singularities*.[10] One of Heidegger's terms

---

[8] Heidegger, *Nietzsche*, vol. III, p. 164, second paragraph.

[9] Heidegger, *Nietzsche*, vol. III, p. 165, second paragraph.

[10] One can ask, however, if Heidegger himself does not ultimately
subscribe to a kind of cyclical history, since he seems to believe that
(1) the pre-Socratic Greek sense of Being as the dynamic interplay of
presence and absence is correct, even though it overlooked the conditions of its own emergence, and (2) that it is possible to return to this
correct interpretation of Being, either (a) *reflectively*, with an appreciation of its importance in the light of the subsequent tradition, or (b)

for these singular, contingent, and unrepeatable transformations in the realm of meaning is *Ereignis*, which means an event, specifically a captivating and enthralling event, an event that catches us up and carries us away, giving everything a new meaning. Heidegger claims that the *Ereignis* also has an aspect of inscrutability:

> Thought concerning truth, in the sense of the essence of *aletheia*, whose essential advent sustains Being and allows it to be sheltered in its belonging to the commencement, is more remote than ever in this last projection of beingness.[11]

Aletheia is the Greek word for truth. The root of *aletheia* is *lethe*, which means *concealment, hiddenness,* or *oblivion.* The prefix "a" in *aletheia* undoes what follows it. Thus *aletheia* means *unconcealment, unhiddenness,* or *undoing oblivion.* But Heidegger also claims that every truth also retains or shelters hiddenness and oblivion within it.

Heidegger's point again is that consciousness cannot be in two places at the same time. Therefore, every new interpretation of Being both reveals something about Being, but it also conceals. First, it conceals *other possible interpretations of Being,* which it rejects as false. Second, it conceals *its own conditions,* for if we are looking at Being under a new interpretation, we are not and cannot also be looking at what makes that interpretation possible.

But in Nietzsche's case, there is a third kind of concealment, for by claiming that his new metaphysics is the overcoming of metaphysics, Nietzsche actually makes overcoming metaphysics more difficult because he fosters the illusion that metaphysics is already overcome, so we don't need to inquire further

---

naïvely, though the liquidation of the present civilization and a return to barbarism, which may be the meaning of Heidegger's famous claim that "only a god can save us now," meaning a return to naïve belief.

11 Heidegger, *Nietzsche,* vol. III, p. 165, third paragraph.

about what metaphysics is and what makes it possible. Nietzsche therefore reinforces our oblivion of what metaphysics is and what makes it possible. But according to Heidegger, the only way to genuinely overcome metaphysics is to think about what makes metaphysics possible. Thus Heidegger writes:

> Inadequate interrogation of the meaning of Nietzsche's doctrine of Return, when viewed in terms of the history of metaphysics, shunts aside the most intrinsic need that is exhibited in the history of Western thought [i.e., the need to understand what makes metaphysics possible]. It thus confirms, by assisting those machinations that are oblivious to Being, the utter abandonment of Being.[12]

It is at this point that we can understand why Heidegger thinks that Nietzsche is not only a metaphysician, but the culmination of metaphysics. Metaphysics thinks about the Being of beings, but it does not think about the meaning of Being, the clearing of Being, etc. Nietzsche is the culmination of metaphysics because Nietzsche not only fails to think about what makes metaphysics possible—what grants different interpretations of Being—he also *makes such thinking altogether impossible* because he fosters the illusion that metaphysics has been finally overcome.

But why does Heidegger believe that we can overcome metaphysics simply by *thinking* about the conditions that make metaphysics possible? To answer this question, we need to look at Heidegger's account of the *specific* metaphysics that he hopes to overcome, namely the metaphysics of the modern technological age, the age of nihilism, in Heidegger's words "the age of consummate meaninglessness."[13]

Consummate meaninglessness is equivalent to the interpretation of Being in terms of man's own subjective needs: Being as certainty, Being as intelligibility, Being as availability and deployability for human purposes. The world is meaningless

---

[12] Heidegger, *Nietzsche*, vol. III, p. 166.
[13] Heidegger, *Nietzsche*, vol. III, p. 174.

because wherever we look, we only encounter projections of our own overweening subjectivity and will to power. The essence of modernity is the idea that everything can be understood and controlled.

This view of the world is made possible by our failure to think about the source of this epoch in the history of Being, i.e., what grants it, what makes it possible. Heidegger claims that:

- ❖ We *cannot understand* the origin of the idea that we can understand everything.
- ❖ We *cannot control* the emergence or departure of the idea that we can control everything.

Trying to understand the origins of nihilism—the conditions that make it possible—forces us to recognize that there is a mystery that cannot be explained or controlled. And this encounter with mystery is alone sufficient to break the spell that everything can be understood and controlled. It is thus a real overcoming of metaphysics and of its culmination in the nihilism of technological modernity.

Counter-Currents, March 19, 2015

LETTING HEIDEGGER BE HEIDEGGER*

Scattered throughout Heidegger's writings are some puzzling distinctions. For instance, in "The Question Concerning Technology," Heidegger claims that the essence (*Wesen*) of technology is nothing technological.[1]

In the lecture "The Danger," Heidegger claims that the essence of death has nothing to do with "hundreds of thousands" dying "*en masse*" in "extermination camps" and man-made famines.[2] The essence of death, in short, is not to be found in actual deaths.

In "Language in the Poem: A Discussion of Georg Trakl's Poems," Heidegger claims that "Anyone who represents pain in terms of sensation remains closed to its essence."[3] In other words, the essence of pain is not to be found in sensations.

In "Language," Heidegger claims that the essence of language is not "an expression and an activity of man."[4] The essence of language, then, is not to be found in actual speech.

In "Building, Dwelling, Thinking," Heidegger claims that "However hard and bitter, however hampering and threatening

---

* I wrote the first draft of this essay in the 1990s when I was in graduate school. The original version was more than twice as long and less than half as meaningful.

[1] Martin Heidegger, "The Question Concerning Technology," in *The Question Concerning Technology and Other Essays*, ed. and trans. William Lovitt (New York: Harper & Row, 1977), p. 4.

[2] Heidegger, *Bremen and Freiburg Lectures: Insight into That Which Is and Basic Principles of Thinking*, trans. Andrew J. Mitchell (Bloomington: Indiana University Press, 2012), p. 53.

[3] Heidegger, "Die Sprache im Gedicht: Eine Erörterung von Georg Trakls Gedicht," *Unterwegs zur Sprache* (Frankfurt: Klostermann, 2018), p. 58; cf. *On the Way to Language*, trans. Peter D. Herz with Joan Stambaugh (New York: Harper & Row, 1971), p. 181.

[4] Heidegger, "Language," in *Poetry, Language, Thought*, ed. and trans. Albert Hofstadter (New York: Harper & Row, 1971), p. 206.

the lack of houses remains, the *real plight of dwelling* does not lie merely in the lack of houses."[5] The essences of dwelling and homelessness are something different than having or lacking a home.

In "The Thing"[6] and the "Memorial Address,"[7] Heidegger claims that the essence of destruction is something different from annihilation by atomic bombs.

Heidegger also asserts some puzzling identities.

For instance, in *Introduction to Metaphysics*, Heidegger claims that Soviet Russia and the United States "are both, metaphysically speaking [i.e., in essence] the same: the same dreary frenzy of unleashed technology [*Technik*] and the regimentation of rootless and normalized men."[8]

In "Das Ge-Stell," Heidegger writes: "Agriculture is now a mechanized food industry, in essence the same [*im Wesen das Selbe*] as the manufacturing of corpses in the gas chambers and extermination camps, the same as the blockading and starving of countries, the same as the production of hydrogen bombs."[9]

What sort of thinking allows Heidegger to draw such distinctions and assert such identities? The answer, of course, is *philosophical* thinking. Drawing a distinction between an entity and its essence is as old as Plato. Once Heidegger asserts a difference between a being and its essence, he is then in a position to assert that different beings are the same "in essence" because they are part of the same historical period. This idea has its roots in the rise of modern philosophical historicism.

In Plato's *Euthyphro*, Socrates asks Euthyphro to spell out the *idea* or the *essence* of piety:

Teach me whatever this idea itself is, so that by gazing at it

---

[5] Heidegger, "Building, Dwelling, Thinking," in *Poetry, Language, Thought*, p. 159.

[6] Heidegger, "The Thing," in *Poetry, Language, Thought*, p. 164.

[7] Heidegger, "Memorial Address," in *Discourse on Thinking*, trans. John M. Anderson and E. Hans Freund (New York: Harper & Row, 1966), esp. p. 56.

[8] Heidegger, *An Introduction to Metaphysics*, trans. Ralph Manheim (New Haven: Yale University Press, 1959), p. 37.

[9] *Bremen and Freiburg Lectures*, p. 27.

and using it as a pattern, I may declare that whatever is like it, among the things you or anyone else may do, is pious, and that whatever is not like it is not pious (6d–e).[10]

Knowing the essence of piety allows us to distinguish pious and impious acts. Pointing to an example of a pious act is not enough, because Socrates wants to know what makes it possible to point out an example of piety in the first place. So the essence of piety is different from pious acts. The essence of piety is neither pious or impious.

The same is true of every other essence. Knowing the essence of dogs allows us to distinguish dogs from foxes. But the essence of dogs is not a particular dog. Knowing the essence of courage allows us to distinguish courage and cowardice. But the essence of courage is not a courageous act.

Or, to put it in general terms: Knowing Being, the essence of what it is to be, allows us to distinguish beings from non-beings. But Being itself is not a being. This, of course Heidegger's famous doctrine of the "ontological difference": "The Being of beings 'is' not itself a being."[11]

The puzzling distinctions listed above are simply examples of the ontological difference: The essence of technology is not a machine; the essence of death is not a particular death; the essence of pain is not a sensation; the essence of language is not speech; the essence of dwelling is not a house; the essence of homelessness is not simply lacking a house; the essence of destruction is not being blown up, and so forth.

But what licenses a philosopher to speak this way? There are experts in every field of phenomena. A philosopher, insofar as he is a philosopher, cannot claim to have greater knowledge than these experts. For instance, philosophers do not know more about living things than biologists. Philosophers know less

---

[10] Plato, *Euthyphro*, in Plato and Aristophanes, *Four Texts on Socrates*, ed. and trans. Thomas G. West and Grace Starry West (Ithaca: Cornell University Press, 1984), p. 48.

[11] Heidegger, *Being and Time*, trans. John Macquarrie and Edward Robinson (New York: Harper & Row, 1962), p. 26.

about healing the sick than doctors. Philosophers know less about strategy than generals and less about courage than infantrymen. Philosophers know less about pain than physiologists, not to mention cancer patients. Philosophers have less expertise about dwelling than people who build houses and about homelessness than those who operate homeless shelters. And so forth.

The expertise of the philosopher lies in taking a step back from all these fields and asking the experts *how* they know what they know. Experts get so involved in straightforwardly knowing and doing particular things that they don't even wonder about *how* they are doing it, or where they as human beings fit into the picture. By talking about the *essences* of technology, death, pain, language, dwelling, and so forth, Heidegger tries to make us wonder about *how the world shows up to us*. That is the job of the philosopher.

Heidegger believed that how the world shows up to us changes from time to time. For the ancient Greeks, things showed up as having an independent existence that eluded our complete understanding and control. For moderns, things show up to us as transparent to our understanding and available for control and consumption. Heidegger called the modern way of seeing the world the *essence* of technology. It is a way of seeing the world that makes modern science and technology possible. This is the basis for Heidegger's claims that the United States and the Soviet Union, or factory farms and extermination camps, are *metaphysically* the same.

Now, a layman might object to Heidegger's views as follows. When Heidegger claims that the essence of homelessness is different from actual homelessness, isn't this just a bit *insensitive* to the homeless? When Heidegger remarks that the essence of pain is different from actual pain, isn't that *insensitive* to people who are actually suffering? If the essence of death is different from actual deaths, even spectacularly horrible deaths, isn't that *insensitive* to everyone who has ever lost a loved one?

But these objections are based on simple misunderstandings. First, when Heidegger mentions extermination camps, manmade famines, mass homelessness, and atomic bombs in the years after the Second World War, he is obviously appealing to *pathos.* He is evoking deep feelings in his audiences, many of whom suffered personally from the very things he names.

But for Heidegger, the task of philosophy is not to console the suffering.[12] That is the work of doctors, priests, therapists, and social workers. Heidegger has no expertise in such matters. Instead, philosophers take a step back from homelessness, pain, and death and raise questions about their *meaning*, their *essences*. That is why people read Heidegger. They don't come to him for a cup of chamomile tea and a shoulder to cry on.

One might also object that claiming that the United States and the Soviet Union are metaphysically the same overlooks the fact that life was *better* in the USA than the USSR. Surely there are lots of important *moral* differences between liberal democracy and communism. Likewise, the claim that factory farms are in essence the same as extermination camps, man-made famines, and hydrogen bombs seems a bit *insensitive* to humans who might resent equating their extermination with pesticides, chemical fertilizers, and feedlots. Isn't there a vast *moral* gulf between using technology to feed millions and using technology to murder millions?

But again, these objections are based on an elementary error. Heidegger is not saying that the US and the USSR, or factory farming and man-made mass death, are *morally* equivalent. He is not, like Isaac Bashevis Singer, claiming that for farm animals, every day is Auschwitz, which is meant as a moral equivalence. Heidegger is saying that these horrors are *metaphysically* equivalent. Moral and metaphysical equivalence are simply two different questions. So claiming that these phenomena are metaphysically the same does not commit one to claiming that they are

---

[12] There is, of course, a long and venerable tradition of philosophers offering consolation in the form of *theodicies*, which argue that human suffering is consistent with the goodness of God. Setting aside the question of whether or not these arguments actually work, the whole exercise seems largely beside the point. For what percentage of the cancer patient's or the grieving parent's suffering focuses on the question of whether God is responsible? The only way such arguments could be any more autistic and irrelevant is if philosophers were to pop up to argue that *they* are not responsible for suffering.

morally the same.

Heidegger is not the clearest writer, but his ideas of the onto-logical difference between beings and Being, and of the stark differences between the Greek and the modern worldviews, can be understood by any moderately intelligent layman. I explained them above in barely a thousand words. So there is really no ex-cuse for Heidegger scholars who ignore these distinctions in or-der to abuse Heidegger in what amounts to politically correct rituals of execration to appease his Leftist critics. Frequently, they sound like they are running for office.

For instance, John D. Caputo calls Heidegger's distinction be-tween the essences and the phenomena of pain, homelessness, and mass death "essentialization." Caputo characterizes essen-tialization as "thoughtless, tasteless, offensive,"[13] "tasteless, in-sensitive, scandalous — thoughtless . . . grotesque and danger-ous,"[14] an "obscenity,"[15] and even a *"reductio ad absurdum"*[16] of Heidegger's thought.

> [Essentialization] accounts for a good deal of Heidegger's habit of saying the most shocking and insensitive — which means unfeeling — things about living things: that real de-structiveness is not found in the universal incineration of all life, human and otherwise, but the loss of a Schwartzwaldi-an *Ding* [Black-Forest thing]; that real homelessness is not a matter of children freezing on winter streets but the loss of a sense of *Wohnen* [dwelling]; that agricultural technology and gas chambers are "essentially the same" . . . It belongs to the essence of Heideggerian *Wesen* [essence] to neutralize the distinction between life and death, to raise itself up to a point of such transcendental purity that it can no longer tell

---

[13] John D. Caputo, "Thinking, Poetry, and Pain," in *Heidegger and Praxis*, ed. Thomas J. Nenon, *The Southern Journal of Philosophy* 27, Supplement (1989), p. 169.

[14] *Ibid*, p. 179.

[15] Caputo, "Incarnation and Essentialization: A Reading of Heidegger," *Philosophy Today*, 35 (1991), p. 41.

[16] *Ibid*.

the difference between agriculture and murder.[17]

The reader already knows enough to respond to this tirade. Caputo is ignoring the difference between *metaphysical* and *moral* sameness. He claims that distinguishing between the *essence* of pain and *sensations* of pain is the same thing as denying that sensations are *real*, which does not follow at all. Caputo accuses Heidegger of *aestheticism*, *asceticism*, and even *anestheticism* (as in anesthesia) for distinguishing between pain and its essence. But Heidegger's real crime is simply being a philosopher. Philosophers do not deny the existence of bodies in pain. They deny only that the *essence* of pain hurts.

For Caputo, however, the crime of being a philosopher is to *reflect* on human suffering—as opposed, I guess, to *doing something* about human suffering. "Doing something" like signaling how much he cares in the pages of philosophy journals:

> What if one were to say that what essentially calls to us in homelessness is not the essence of dwelling but the cries of those who suffer from lack of shelter? What if the call were really a cry of grief? What if the call were the appeal for help of those who suffer? What if the summons by which were are summarily called were the summons for aid by the victim? What if responding to the appeal of the victim were the oldest responsibility of all?[18]

This, of course, is a legitimate response to human suffering. It is also the *first* response to human suffering. It is the response of concerned citizens, global humanitarians, policemen, firemen, emergency medical technicians, doctors, nurses, priests, therapists, councilors, and social workers. But it is not the *philosophical* response to suffering, which first and foremost is to *understand*. Thus Caputo's indictment of Heidegger is basically that he chose to be a philosopher, not a social worker.

Note that Caputo does not claim that distinguishing between

---

[17] *Ibid*, pp. 40–41.
[18] Caputo, "Thinking, Poetry, and Pain," p. 272.

the essence of language and human speech denies the reality of human speech. Nor does it trigger torrents of abuse. Caputo is only focusing on emotional hot-button issues: pain, homelessness, mass death. Thus his position is basically that only these issues should be off limits to philosophical reflection, because to philosophize about the greatest problems facing humanity is somehow in bad taste.

When reading some of Heidegger's more pedestrian-minded detractors, one often wonders: Why Heidegger? What attracted them to Heidegger in the first place? For instance, Richard Rorty writes:

> One might think that the destruction of the earth and the standardization of man were bad enough . . . without bringing in the world of the spirit at all. But this would be to treat "forgetfulness of being" as just a handy label for whatever it is that has been going wrong lately . . . This way of putting things may suggest that I am, like a good modern, neglecting the "ontological difference" between Being and beings. But [when talking about the problems of modernity] Heidegger neglected it too—and it is well for him that he does.[19]

Heidegger evoked the crises of the post-War age to draw people into his philosophical reflections. Then he asked them to *take a step back* from engagement with the problems of the world and *reflect a bit on their meaning*. But, as Heidegger himself pointed out, to dispense with the reflective turn and leave it at "Mankind has entered the atomic age" is not to rise above the platitudes of illustrated newsmagazines.[20] For Rorty, though, that is all well and good. So why Heidegger?

Years ago, I submitted an essay on Nietzsche to a philosophy

---

[19] Richard Rorty, "Overcoming the Tradition: Heidegger and Dewey," *Consequences of Pragmatism: Essays 1972–1980* (Minneapolis: University of Minnesota Press, 1982), p. 48.

[20] Heidegger, *The Principle of Reason*, trans. Reginald Lilly (Bloomington: Indiana University Press, 1991), pp. 121–24.

journal. It was rejected, and when I read the peer reviewer's report, it was clear that he actually had no objections to my discussion of Nietzsche—beyond the fact that he would have preferred that I had written a paper on John Rawls instead. This is a very common vice in academia. Instead of criticizing a writer for what he has actually written, he is attacked for not writing what his critic would have preferred he had written. They want to change the subject. But they don't just come out and say so, because then they would have no actual grounds on which to criticize you.

Caputo and Rorty don't really want to engage Heidegger philosophically. They simply wish he were someone else, someone more like them. Philosophy, however, is fundamentally different from *passionate engagement* with the problems of mankind. Philosophy begins with *reflective disengagement* and then *ponders the meanings* of things, even things that we would like to abolish, like pain, homelessness, and mass murder.

But what if this reflective turn reveals that the deep metaphysical assumptions of liberal democracy are the same as communist and fascist totalitarianism? And what if allowing these assumptions to go unchallenged dooms liberal democracy into becoming nothing more than a soft totalitarian dystopia?

This is why Heidegger matters. This is why even academic Leftists who would prefer to simply change the subject and focus on politics need to take a step back and reflect on the meaning of what they are doing. Philosophical reflection itself changes nothing. But we can't philosophize forever. We have to return to life. And when we do, philosophy allows us to see the world, its problems, and our tasks in a new light. And seeing the world anew can change everything. This is why we need to let Heidegger be Heidegger.

Counter-Currents, September 26, 2018

HEIDEGGER & ETHNIC NATIONALISM*

Martin Heidegger, the most celebrated and influential philosopher of the twentieth century, was an ethnic nationalist—and not just any old ethnic nationalist, but a supporter of German National Socialism. Moreover, Heidegger's National Socialism was not merely the superficial infatuation of a politically naïve intellectual. Instead, it was a logical outgrowth of his philosophy. Which means that today's nationalists can draw upon the most formidable thinker of our time to deepen, sharpen, and defend the ethnonationalist idea.

The kinds of political order that men create are based on their fundamental worldview: their sense of who they are, where they fit into the world, what is right and wrong, and what is politically possible. These are the questions of "metapolitics": those things that come before the political, i.e., the intellectual and cultural presuppositions of political orders. Modern globalism follows from modern man's self-image and ethos. Modern man is rootless and cosmopolitan. Modern man is individualistic. Modern man uses science and technology to pursue the mastery and possession of nature.

These three traits are beautifully illustrated in the opening pages of Ayn Rand's novel *The Fountainhead*.[1] Howard Roark, the novel's hero, has just been expelled from architecture school, basically because all he cared about learning was the science and technology of construction. He rejected the aesthetic tradition of architecture because he had his own vision. Supremely confident he can go it alone, he laughs off the setback and goes swimming.

Rand describes Roark standing on a cliff overlooking his swimming hole. The water is still, so the rock is doubled by its reflection. There is blue sky above and blue sky below, so the

---

* Lecture delivered at The London Forum on Saturday, May 27, 2017.
[1] Ayn Rand, *The Fountainhead* (New York: Bobbs-Merrill, 1943).

rock appears to be floating in space. Then Rand adds an interesting little detail. Instead of the man standing on the rock jutting out of the earth, it appears that the rock is floating in space, "anchored to the feet of the man."

Roark does not laugh when he looks at the world around him. He does not see the living rock. He sees building stones. He does not see trees. He sees lumber. He sees the word as nothing more than a stockpile of resources to be appropriated and remade according to human plans—his plans. "These rocks, he thought, are waiting for me; waiting for the drill, the dynamite and my voice; waiting to be split, ripped, pounded, reborn; waiting for the shape my hands will give them."

Howard Roark is rootless: he does not stand on the earth. Instead, the earth is just a big ball of natural resources floating through the void anchored to him. Howard Roark is an individualist. He rejects tradition in favor of his own "unborrowed" vision. Finally, Howard Roark uses science and technology to master and transform nature according to his designs.

How do cosmopolitan man, individualist man, and technological man all hang together? Do they spring from a common root? The answer is yes, and it is a deep root, teaching all the way back to the origins of Western philosophy and natural science in ancient Greece.

In traditional societies, the notions of order do not differentiate between the human and the natural worlds. The Chinese talk about the *tao*, which is the "way" of both natural and human things. The same is true of the Greek notion of *nomos*, from which our ideas of the laws of men and the laws of nature derive.

The early Greek natural philosophers, however, noticed that there was a difference between the ways of the natural and the human worlds. Human ways of life—languages and customs—vary from place to place (meaning that men have different cultures) and from time to time (meaning that cultures have histories). Human ways of life are particular, not universal. They are not unchanging, but Protean and restless and hard to pin down.

Nature, by contrast, was the same everywhere, and it changes so slowly that the Greeks thought it never changed at all, just

went through endless cycles. The early Greek natural philosophers believed that the universal is better than the particular, the
unchanging is better than the changing, and cyclical change is
better than non-cyclical change (including "progress"). Nature's
laws are better than human laws. Nature allows certitude and
predictability, whereas human customs lack these advantages.
Thus the early Greek natural philosophers replaced the old idea
of the way of things with a distinction between *nature*, which is
universal and unchanging, and *convention*, which is particular
and mutable—varying from time to time and place to place,
never repeating or returning to the same. And they held that nature is better than convention, thus we should guide our lives by
nature and not convention.

Consequently, the beginning of the philosophical life is to
take an inventory of the human condition. When we do this, we
discover that there is a human *nature*, unchanging and common
to all men—such as our bodily desires—and a crust of conventions that vary from time to time and place to place and that
were taught to us by the people around us long before we were
self-conscious, much less capable of exercising critical reason.
These conventions include language, myths, and morals, some
that help and others that hinder our ability to live according to
our nature.

To become a philosopher, we must free out minds from prejudices—from beliefs that we have uncritically accepted from our
society. Plato likened society—the world of authoritative shared
opinions—to a cave in which shackled prisoners are forced to
watch the equivalent of an Indonesian shadow-puppet play and
mistake it for reality. He likened the process of becoming a philosopher to liberating oneself from the prison of the cave of opinion and toiling upward to the surface of the Earth where one can
live in the sunlit world of truth.

The beginnings of individualism and cosmopolitanism are
basically the same: to obtain objective knowledge of universal,
unchanging nature, one must liberate one's mind from the realm
of opinion or custom, which are inherently social, meaning that
they are shared by a whole community. One must, in an important sense, cease to be a citizen of one's homeland, for a citi-

zen believes that the traditions of his homeland are authoritative. But if the philosopher is not a citizen of Athens or England,
what is his homeland? When Diogenes the Cynic, who was born
in Sinope, was asked the name of his hometown—his *polis*—he
did not say that he was a citizen of Sinope, but a citizen of the
world. The cosmos was his *polis*, from which we get the word
cosmopolitan.[2] To say that one is a cosmopolitan is to say that
one is an emancipated individual who lives by reason in accordance with nature, which is universal and unchanging.

How does cosmopolitan and individualist man become technological man? The common root of all three is the use of reason,
emancipated from social prejudice, to gain knowledge of nature.
Once the cosmopolitan individual decides to take his bearings
from reason and nature rather than custom and convention, he
looks within and finds his natural human desires for food, com-
fort, security, etc. Then he looks around nature with unblinkered
eyes for ways to satisfy himself. Having discarded any merely
social conventions, he has no impediments to gratifying his
wishes at the expense of nature. Scientific and technological
progress was up and running.

Two other attitudes allied with the quest for objective
knowledge feed into technological progress.

First, just as the philosopher looks below the crust of opinion
to get to the truth of nature, the scientist looks below the surface
of nature—and the myriad natural kinds—to find a few simple
underlying natural laws that allow him to better understand and
transform nature according to his will. Thus to the scientist, the
natural world we see around us looks more and more provisional. It looks increasingly like a stockpile of resources for human projects.

Second, the Will to Power is implicit in the very notion of objective knowledge. For why prefer the universal and unchanging
to the particular and protean? Because the universal and unchanging is secure. You can always count on it. Thus it provides
a secure foundation for our plans. There is a well-founded cliché

---

[2] See my essay "What's Wrong with Cosmopolitanism?," *In Defense of Prejudice* (San Francisco: Counter-Currents, 2017).

about ugly Americans abroad going to McDonald's rather than eating the local cuisine. But there is a logic to it, because the food at McDonald's is universal and unchanging, so you always know what to expect. That is why I *don't* eat the food at MacDonald's, but I do stop in to use the toilets, because you can always count on clean restrooms as well. The driving force of objective conceptions of knowledge was a subjective desire for certitude and control that, over time, gave rise to such ideas as Platonic and Aristotelian forms, Cartesian representations, and eventually the operationalization of science in terms of technical feats of prediction and control.

But what if, as Heidegger argues, the primary source of *meaning* in life and the primary source of moral and aesthetic *measure* is our *participation* in the worlds of shared custom and opinion — in various ethnic communities — the very things that cosmopolitan, individualist, and technological man is concerned to leave behind? Heidegger's answer is that a world deprived of meaning and measure will become a world of unbounded nihilism — nihilism spreading out in all directions.

A world without measure is also a world without borders and boundaries. It is a world in which distinct nations and races will disappear, for liberation from particular collective identities is the toll we pay to play the whole cosmopolitan game, and if the satisfaction of our desires is what life is all about, why let racial differences constrict your potential dating and mating pool?

But the universal, homogeneous global state will be no utopia. What is the meaning of life for cosmopolitan-individualist-technological man? Basically to appropriate, transform, and consume nature. And doing so without measure leads to what Heidegger called "the gigantic" (*das Riesige*): the realm of exploding populations, of cities surging upwards, plunging downwards, and sprawling out in all directions — a world where the new is always improved and more is always better — a world where knowing that you *can* do something is equivalent to knowing that you *should* do it — a world of an ever-expanding humanoid biomass, throbbing, swarming, and pullulating over the globe — until, at last, we crash into objective limits that we refused to see and factor into our plans, and the earth becomes a scorched boneyard, in which some of the skeletons enjoyed the privilege of a long string of numbers in their bank accounts before the lights blinked out forever and the world returned to being just lifeless matter in space.

If the beginning of Western philosophy and science are leading to that end, maybe it is time for a new beginning. In 1930, Heidegger began to think that the National Socialist movement was just the new beginning or inception (*Anfang*) he had hoped for. National Socialism stood for rootedness in a particular homeland, language, and tradition, as opposed to cosmopolitan rootlessness and the beep beep, boop boop of machine communication and the cha-ching of commerce, which are the true universal languages. National Socialism was about collectivism over individualism, the common good before individual interests. And National Socialism was very, very "green," seeking to preserve nature and human-scale living from the depredations of industrialization and giantism. Thus in 1935, Heidegger declared in one of lectures that the "inner truth and greatness" of National Socialism was based on "the confrontation of global technology and modern man."[3]

Heidegger eventually became disillusioned with National Socialism. He came to see it not as the new beginning for which he hoped, but as just another form of modern technological nihilism. After the war, he promoted the myth that his support of National Socialism was just the blunder of a naïve and essentially apolitical thinker. We were supposed to believe that Heidegger was just a political Thales, who fell down a well while gazing at the heavens.

But nothing could be further from the truth. Heidegger's philosophy was always political—and specifically ethnonationalist—both before and after the Third Reich, although after the war he took pains to obscure this fact. After the war, Heidegger largely refrained from speaking about political topics, but as a

---

[3] Martin Heidegger, *Introduction to Metaphysics*, trans. Gregory Fried and Richard Polt (New Haven: Yale University Press, 2000), p. 213.

philosopher he patiently laid the metapolitical conditions for a new post-totalitarian critique of cosmopolitanism, individualism, and technological nihilism. In short, Heidegger was one of the founders of what we today call the New Right.

Heidegger's *magnum opus* is *Being and Time*, which was published in 1927. *Being and Time* is an implicitly political work, rife with the language of the Conservative Revolutionary movement, including its valorization of the Front experience of the First World War as a model for a new ethic of hardness, seriousness, and solidarity, as well as its condemnation of the hedonism, selfishness, and shallow social conformism of Weimar.

But the politics of *Being and Time* goes much deeper, for it attacks the very root of cosmopolitan-individualist-technological man, namely the idea of objective knowledge emancipated from the realm of collective opinion.

This is not the occasion to delve into technical philosophical arguments. But Heidegger's conclusion is that all cognitive activities—even those of philosophy and science—are made possible by language and other social practices that are learned ultimately by participation in a community that is particular, not universal—changing, not eternal—provincial, not cosmopolitan. In other words, at the root of every cognitive act is ethnic identity. In Heidegger's words, "I believe that there is no essential work of the spirit that does not have its root in originary autochthony."[4] Thus, contrary to Plato and other Greek philosophers, deracination is not the path to wisdom but the path to the folly of nihilism, which is playing itself out today on the global stage.

One expression of the cosmopolitan ambition of classical philosophy is to leave human languages behind and find a universal, objective form of communication. Heidegger's thought is so fundamentally opposed to cosmopolitanism that he declared that the two truly philosophical languages were ancient Greek and German. Heidegger believed that thought is a gift of language and culture. One needs a certain cultural and linguistic

---

4 Martin Heidegger, *Reden und andere Zeugnisse eines Lebensweges (1910–1976), Gesamtausgabe*, vol. 16, ed. Hermann Heidegger (Frankfurt: Klostermann, 2000), p. 551.

heritage to spy the fundamental truths necessary to launch a new philosophical age. The Greek language and culture gave us the beginning of Western philosophy. German language and culture gave us a new beginning, and, starting in 1930, Heidegger believed that National Socialism might carry out the new beginning of thought on the cultural and political plane, bringing an end to the modern world.

If even philosophy is a product of language and culture, does that mean that Greek philosophy is only true for Greeks, and German philosophy is only true for Germans? No, Heidegger is not that kind of relativist. Seeing new truths requires a certain viewpoint, but once discovered such truths are true for everyone. Only the Greeks could have launched the first inception of Western thought, but it spread to all of Europe and then encompassed the globe. Likewise, even though only the Germans could have created the new inception, it is true for all of us and has the potential to transform all life on earth.

Greek philosophy was a product of the Greek language and culture. But it overlooked its own contingent and particular origins. The Greek objective conception of knowledge presented an image of man uprooted from language, customs, and place, a citizen of the world. The consummation of the first inception is modern technological civilization, in which man thinks of himself as entirely rootless and thinks of the world as merely a stockpile of resources to be manipulated and ultimately consumed. By contrast, the German new beginning will lead Western man back to rootedness, an acceptance of finitude and uncertainty, and a sense that we are part of the natural world, charged with being its guardians, not its exploiters and consumers.

How then did the Germans give rise to a new beginning for philosophy? For Heidegger, a new inception changes the meaning of everything. It is a pervasive change in the *Zeitgeist* that cannot be ascribed to particular thinkers. Instead, individual thinkers are merely responding to and articulating a change that transcends any individual mind.

At the core of the new inception is a sense of what the German Idealists called the finitude and historical conditionedness of consciousness. Kant argued that our knowledge of reality is limited to what can be given to our finite cognitive faculties. Hegel and Heidegger argued that the finite conditions of consciousness include linguistic and cultural practices that vary from time to time and place to place. Unlike the first inception, in which consciousness tries to make itself absolute by emancipating itself from history, culture, language, and "prejudice" in order to comprehend its own origins, the new inception argues that this is impossible. Consciousness cannot comprehend its own origins. The Kantian categories are just there. The contingencies of language and culture are just there. You can't get behind them to explain them.

Greek philosophy thinks of knowledge as an objective, "God's-eye" view of the world and thus sees rootedness and participation in particular languages and cultures as an impediment to knowing the world. German philosophy rejects the idea that human knowledge should be measured by an inhuman standard of objectivity and thus sees rootedness and participation in particular languages and cultures as a necessary condition for the kind of knowledge that is possible for humans to achieve: a finite, human's-eye view of the world.

Not all languages, cultures, and individual perspectives are equal. Some conceal more than they reveal. But to win the kind of truth that is available to man, we have to replace bad perspectives with better ones, crude languages with subtler ones, primitive cultures with advanced ones—not try to chuck language, culture, and perspective altogether for a chimerical conception of objectivity. Finite, perspectival human knowledge may be rife with uncertainty and constantly subject to revision and growth, but for all its imperfections, it is the only kind of knowledge we have ever had, and it has been good enough to create both the wonders and the horrors of the modern world.

Heidegger's opposition to cosmopolitanism in *Being and Time* is so adamant and systematic that he does not even talk about human beings, which is a universal notion. Nor does he talk about man as the "rational animal," which is just a composite of two universal notions. Instead, Heidegger speaks of *"Dasein,"* which is a German word for existence, but it is usually left untranslated in Heidegger's texts because he uses it as a technical term. Pick up any Heidegger book, and turn to a random page. Chances are, you will see *Dasein* with a capital "D."

Heidegger hears "*Dasein*" as a composite of "*Da*" (there) and "*Sein*" (being). So *Dasein* means "being there." For Heidegger, we are not rootless citizens of the world. We are *Dasein*, a being who is essentially rooted in a particular language, culture, and place. Contra Plato, Heidegger does not think of the "*Da*"—our language, culture, and place—as first and foremost a *prison* that prevents us from knowing the real world. Instead, he sees the "*Da*" as what *enables* us to access the world in the first place. *Dasein* is always sometime and someplace, but his world opens out in all directions and into the past and the future. *Dasein* is inherently parochial, not cosmopolitan. *Dasein* is no abstract or atomized individual but a concrete individual rooted in a shared language and culture. Note well that this is true even of self-declared cosmopolitans, individualists, and technological supermen. What's the difference between us and them? They too have roots, but they are just in denial about them. Cosmopolitan, individualist, technological man is also fake, phony, inauthentic man.

Authenticity means being honest with yourself about your identity and living accordingly. For Heidegger, we cannot construct our identities. We cannot invent, much less reinvent, ourselves. We cannot choose who we are. Instead, our identities are handed to us by our language, culture, and lineage. For Heidegger, freedom comes in only in what we do with the identity that is given us. Our most fundamental choice is whether we own up to our identity or deny it. Authenticity is owning up to who we are. Inauthenticity is refusing to own up to our identity and instead living according to fantasies about who we are, fantasies projected by ourselves or others.

Whether we choose authenticity or inauthenticity, we remain the same person, but in radically different states. The authentic person lives according to his nature, which the Greeks defined as well-being (*eudaimonia*). The inauthentic person lives contrary to his nature and thus lacks well-being.

For Heidegger, being a German ethnic nationalist, rather than a cosmopolitan liberal or Communist, was simply a matter of authenticity, of owning up to his ethnic identity—his particular linguistic and cultural "*Da*"—and living accordingly. And when the world opposes you living according to your nature, well-being requires self-assertion. If others push you around, you have to push back. You have to take your own side in a fight.

The linguistic and cultural aspects of our identities are learned from infancy on. They are our "second nature." But what of our genetic lineage, our "first nature"? What role does biological race play in Heidegger's thought? Heidegger did not deny that biological race was real, but he was uncomfortable with the importance ascribed to it by the National Socialists. For Heidegger, being white was a *necessary* but not *sufficient* condition for German identity.[5] All Germans are white, but not all whites are German.

Being a German, Heidegger's primary concern was German ethnic nationalism, and he believed that an over-emphasis on biological race undermined German ethnic identity. For Heidegger, emphasizing the white race posed the same danger as emphasizing the human race. Both are universals that undermine specific cultural identities. "There's only one race, the human race," is a slogan trotted out to undermine the particular identities of all races and nations, to break down the barriers that maintain diversity and promote pan-mixia, with the end result of global homogeneity.

But the idea that "There's only one race that matters, the white race," promotes the same breakdown of barriers between white ethnic groups, the same mixing and erasure of identity. And when the Second World War began, and different peoples fell under German control, the logic of biological racism led them quite naturally to the idea of assimilating biologically similar Europeans into the German Reich, which would inevitably erode the cultural integrity of conqueror and conquered alike.

So for Heidegger, biological race is important. To say that whiteness is a necessary condition of any European identity is to

---

[5] Martin Heidegger, *Ponderings II–VI*, trans. Richard Rojcewicz (Bloomington: Indiana University Press, 2014), notebook III, section 195, p. 139.

give race a far greater importance than accepted by the civic nationalists and multiculturalists of today. But by the same token,
biological race is not the whole of any European identity, and
mistaking a part for the whole is profoundly subversive of ethnic identity.

Thus, while it was true to say that Heidegger was a white
man, it was truer still to say that he was a German, even more
true to say that he was a Black Forest Swabian of peasant stock,
but truest of all to say that he was a Heidegger, born of the union of Friedrich Heidegger and Johanna Kempf. But it was only
the very specific mixture of their genes that gave us the brain of
Martin Heidegger—as opposed to those of his brother or his sis-
ter. And once that piece of hardware was programmed with the
software of Martin Heidegger's particular language, culture, and
experiences, new philosophical prospects opened up that we
will be exploring for centuries to come.

We have seen how Heidegger's conception of who we are
undermines both cosmopolitanism and individualism by arguing that every human act—even the heroic striving to uproot
oneself from tradition—is rooted in a particular language, culture, and identity, and our only choice in this matter is to own
up to this fact or to continue to delude ourselves about it. But
how does Heidegger undermine man, the conqueror of nature?
Heidegger teaches us that we are finite. He forces us to confront
the fact that we are not self-defining, self-creating beings. We are
defined by forces outside our ken or control. He shows us that
the very idea that underlies the modern conquest of nature—
namely that we can know everything and control everything—is
not something we can either understand or control. It is, instead,
a mania that enthralls us. It is a mysterious something that came
up behind us, reft us up by the nape of our necks, and is speed-
ing us forward toward the planetary boneyard. There's a real
sense in which we do not have technology, technology has us.

But once we realize that we can't understand why we think
we can understand everything, and we can't control the idea
that we think we can control everything—once we see that the
conquest of nature is a collective mania that arises from inscrutable sources—the spell is broken. Once our hubris is humbled

before the mystery of our origins—once our Faustian strivings are contained within classical limits—we will once again see the earth as our home. And although we will strive to make the earth a safe and comfortable dwelling place, we will no longer think of ourselves as cosmopolitan nomads, slashing and burning—or swindling and looting—then moving on to greener pastures. We can even have our computers and smart phones and machines that go "ping." But they will no longer have us.

So I bring you good news. Martin Heidegger, one of the most formidable thinkers of our time, was an ethnonationalist who offers enormous metapolitical resources to the fight of all peoples against globalization. With Heidegger's help, we rootless phony cosmopolitans can rediscover who we really are and dwell authentically on Earth once more.

Counter-Currents, June 27 & July 5, 2017

RICHARD POLT'S
TIME & TRAUMA

Richard Polt
Time and Trauma: Thinking Through Heidegger in the Thirties
New York: Rowman & Littlefield, 2019

Richard Polt is one of the most distinguished and prolific Heidegger scholars active today. He is the author of one of the best introductory books on Heidegger, *Heidegger: An Introduction,* as well as a commentary on one of Heidegger's most difficult texts, *The Emergency of Being: On Heidegger's "Contributions to Philosophy."*[1] He has also edited and translated at least ten books, alone or in collaboration. And he is the author of dozens of essays, reviews, and shorter translations.

Polt's *Time and Trauma* is the best book yet written on Heidegger's philosophy and politics during the Third Reich.

Books on Heidegger's politics basically fall into two categories: offensive and defensive. Anti-Heideggerians like Emmanuel Faye and Ronald Beiner generally disagree with Heidegger's philosophy and wish to diminish his influence by creating a moral panic about the contagions of Nazism and anti-Semitism, so that timid professors will be hesitant to read and teach Heidegger. Heideggerians like Polt wish to defend Heidegger's core ideas—and their own academic careers—from the stigma promoted by people like Faye and Beiner. Both groups, of course, never entertain the possibility that Heidegger's ideas on politics might have some inner truth and greatness.

Polt offers a novel argument for critically engaging rather than merely dismissing Heidegger's political ideas:

The challenge is not just to interpret Heidegger but to

---

[1] Richard Polt, *Heidegger: An Introduction* (Ithaca: Cornell University Press, 1997) and *The Emergency of Being: On Heidegger's "Contributions to Philosophy"* (Ithaca: Cornell University Press, 2006).

think and act today. The twenty-first century is witnessing a disturbing resurgence of neofascist movements, complete with an intelligentsia that draws on right-wing theorists of the past, including Heidegger. To denounce these developments in the name of morality and liberal democracy is correct and necessary, in my view, but this is no answer to the ideas of those who reject these standpoints. A more adequate and philosophical response goes through Heidegger to grasp the theoretical inadequacies of his stances toward politics, and to show that his best insights of the thirties can be appropriated in support of a pluralistic and free society. (p. 7)

Later Polt writes: "[Heidegger's] metaphysical diagnosis of Nazism is certainly debatable, but that is a debate worth having, and perhaps a necessary one if today's racist or neofascist movements are to be combatted intellectually" (p. 195).

In a note, Polt explains who these "neofascist" intellectuals are: "Heidegger is a popular figure on counter-currents.com, home of Counter-Currents Publishing, purveyor of books by racists and neofascists. In Russia, political theorist Alexander Dugin has enlisted Heidegger in his project of a 'Eurasianism' that is profoundly antiliberal, although he denies that it is fascist" (p. 250, n15). Although Polt does not mention me by name, I am the primary person at *Counter-Currents* writing about Heidegger and political philosophy. Naturally, I am flattered that one of the express purposes of Polt's book is to intellectually combat people like me. But I was a bit worried he might actually score some points. Hence this review.

In his first chapter, "Into the Happening of Being," Polt explains how Heidegger's writings in the 1930s emerge from *Being and Time*, his unfinished *magnum opus* published in 1927. Chapter 2, "Passing Through the Political," spans 111 pages and surveys all the relevant texts, many of them recently published, including the first five volumes of the *Black Notebooks*. Chapter 3, "Recovering Politics," is a critique of Heidegger's politics in which Polt argues that his own liberal-democratic political preferences are consistent with Heidegger's philosophy. Chapter 4,

"Toward Traumatic Ontology," seeks to restate what he thinks is of permanent value in Heidegger's ideas of the 1930s. Because of considerations of space, I will focus primarily on chapters 1–3.

Time and Trauma has many virtues. Polt's scholarship is exhaustive, his prose is fairly lucid (although not as clear as his first two Heidegger books), and his treatment of Heidegger's most controversial statements is scrupulous and level-headed. But I don't find his defense of liberal democracy very convincing.

In 1927, Heidegger published *Being and Time* prematurely and under duress. *Being and Time* was planned to be in two parts, each with three divisions. The published book consists of the first two divisions of part one, i.e., one third of the total outline. But Heidegger needed to get a book into print to be promoted to full professor at the University of Marburg, so he took what he had written thus far and sent it to Edmund Husserl, who published it as a volume of his journal, *Yearbook for Phenomenology and Phenomenological Research*.

Then in 1928, Heidegger was offered Husserl's chair of philosophy at the University of Freiburg, where he remained for the rest of his career. His career was secure, but the unfinished business of *Being and Time* would hang over his head for years to come, and today there is an academic cottage industry speculating about the relationship of Heidegger's later work to the unfinished outline of *Being and Time*.

Being and Time is a work of phenomenology, meaning that it describes the different ways in which objects become present to us. It is also classified as "hermeneutic" phenomenology, because Heidegger claims that all things show up as meaningful. Heidegger uses the word "Being" (*Sein*) to refer to meaningful presence.

Heidegger calls his book *Being and Time* because he claims that "time" is the context or "horizon" of Being. Objects show up as meaningful in terms of our projects for the future, which are in turn based upon our pasts: our language, culture, historical situation, and individual life courses. This sense of "time" is obviously a specifically human phenomenon. If one uses "time" in the ordinary sense of the world, it makes sense to speak about a time before human beings, and human time, existed.

Heidegger claims that man and meaning depend on one another. Meaning cannot exist without man, and man cannot exist without meaning. In the published portion of *Being and Time*, Heidegger deals with the man-meaning relationship from the point of view of man: how meaning depends upon us. Thus *Being and Time* has a "transcendental" feel. Like Kant and Husserl, Heidegger describes the universal structures and activities of consciousness that allow things to show up as meaningful.

In the third division of part one of *Being and Time*, Heidegger planned to approach the man-meaning relationship from the side of meaning, showing how man depends on meaning, specifically meanings that transcend the individual mind. Systems of *collective* meaning like language and culture loom up over us as authoritative powers, enthrall us, enter into us, shape our consciousness, and open up worlds of meaning.

If the extant parts of *Being and Time* had a Kantian flavor, with its talk of universal structures of consciousness, the unwritten parts would have had a Hegelian flavor, focusing instead on historically *contingent* and *mutable* forms of meaning. This focus characterizes Heidegger's subsequent publications.

In Heidegger's words, his approach was shifting "from the understanding of being to the *happening of being*" (quoted in Polt, p. 1). In other words: shifting from the knower's understanding of meaning to the historical happening of meaning which shapes the knower. In Polt's words, "The emphasis is no longer on our constitution—human nature, in traditional terms—but on a transformative event that seizes us and thrusts us into the condition of 'being-there' (*Dasein*)" (p. 2). "*Dasein*" is Heidegger's term for the human knower who is constituted by a particular *there*: a particular time and place. *Dasein* is a historical being's particular point of view, not a disembodied subjectivity.

A more ordinary sense of "world" is "everything": all things, including us, whether we know about them or not, i.e., the universe. When Heidegger speaks of world, however, he means something more akin to the "art world" or the "sports world," i.e., not just a realm of things, but multiple realms of *meaningful* things.

Meaningful to whom? To us. To *Dasein*. The universe can exist without human knowers. But the art world cannot. *Dasein* makes worlds of meaning possible. "With *Dasein*, world first happens. *Dasein* breaks in, and beings are revealed" (quoted in Polt, p. 29). Before there was *Dasein*, there was just a universe, immense but meaningless, not worlds of meaning.

Since meaning is structured in terms of time, Heidegger also speaks of the creation of worlds of meaning as the emergence of time: "the moment when time opens itself up in its dimensions" and is "torn open into present, past, and future" (quoted in Polt, p. 23).

Heidegger wasn't really interested in the emergence of *Dasein* and worlds of meaning within *natural* history. Instead, in the 1930s, his primary focus is on *fundamental changes of meaning within human history*. Heidegger uses two main words to describe these changes of meaning: *Anfang* (beginning, inception) and *Ereignis* (event). Heidegger's primary concern is not with the history of *things* but the history of *meaning*.

Nor is Heidegger primarily concerned with the meanings of particular things to particular people, but rather with *global* meanings, *the meaning of everything to everyone*. These global meanings are the stuff of metaphysics. Changes in global meanings are fundamental breaks in human history, such as the division of history into BC and AD, or between the Middle Ages and the Renaissance, or between the age of Enlightenment and the ages of unreason that came before.

Such fundamental changes in meaning often accompany crises, in which settled orders of meaning break down in the face of realities they cannot grasp, and new meanings emerge. These crises of meaning implicate us as well. They are crises of *identity*.

All of these ideas form the groundwork for Heidegger's political involvement. In the 1930s, Heidegger spoke of two inceptions: the first Greek, the second German. The first inception was the beginning of Western philosophy in ancient Greece, which gave rise to the idea of objective knowledge unconditioned by the contingencies of time and place. Philosophy is a view from nowhere. Its homeland is no particular *polis*, but rather the cosmos, hence the idea of cosmopolitanism.[2] Heidegger treats the second inception as still outstanding, but in truth it began with the German idealist tradition, which stressed that consciousness is finite and historically conditioned, a view from somewhere. *Dasein* is the finite, historically conditioned knower.

The first inception led, ultimately, to the rise of cosmopolitanism and technological civilization. But Heidegger believed that this civilization was entering a crisis, namely nihilism. Heidegger held that meaning ultimately derives from rootedness in a particular culture and language. The first inception's idea of objective knowledge destroys such roots, ushering in an age of nihilism. To overcome nihilism, we ultimately need a new inception: a culture and a politics that do justice to man's finitude and rootedness in concrete ways of life.

This is why Heidegger embraced National Socialism in 1930. In 1933, after Hitler assumed power, Heidegger joined the party and became Rector of the University of Freiburg, where he was charged with implementing National Socialist educational reforms. Heidegger was an enthusiastic but unorthodox National Socialist. His tenure as Rector was stressful and racked by conflict with his colleagues and superiors. He stepped down after a year and returned to full-time teaching.

Polt's chapter on Heidegger's politics in the 1930s is so rich that it defies summary. It is the best part of his book and should be read by anyone with a serious interest in this topic.

Heidegger's political thought basically went through two phases. Early on, Heidegger was what one might call a *humanistic historicist*. He was *historicist* because he believed that our thought is rooted in concrete historical traditions and ways of life. He was a *humanist* because, following Nietzsche, he believed that great philosophers, poets, and statesmen create these traditions and ways of life. His hope was that National Socialism would bring about a new inception, legislating a new culture and way of life.

---

[2] See Greg Johnson, "What's Wrong with Cosmopolitanism?," *In Defense of Prejudice* (San Francisco: Counter-Currents, 2017).

This viewpoint is, however, implicitly totalitarian and nihilistic. Creating a new culture means setting up new standards of truth and goodness. Which means that such decisions are unconstrained by prior standards of truth and goodness. This implies that the legislator can do anything he wishes and call it true or good.

In practical terms, Heidegger's view is indistinguishable from Stalinism, which declares the Communist Party and its leaders oracles of truth and goodness, since they are the vanguard of the historical process, which in effect means that the true and good are whatever the state *says* they are, as long it is expedient.

Later, as Heidegger became disillusioned with Nietzsche and National Socialism, he came to see humanistic historicism as another form of nihilism and unbounded technological machination. Heidegger's mature philosophy is resolutely anti-humanist. Human subjectivity is not "behind" history, not even the subjectivity of great men. Rather, history is "behind" human subjectivity. Which means that human beings cannot take control over our own destinies and change the course of history. That is the error of all forms of modern technological nihilism, including National Socialism. Instead, we can only wait as modern nihilism burns itself out and a new inception emerges.

Heidegger sums up the course of his thinking in a 1939 entry in his *Black Notebooks*:

> Thinking purely "metaphysically" (that is, in terms of the history of beyng [a translation of the archaic German spelling "*Seyn*"], during the years 1930–1934, I saw in National Socialism the possibility of a transition into another inception and gave it this interpretation. Thereby I mistook and underestimated this "movement" in its authentic forces and inner necessities as also in the extent and the kind of its greatness. Instead, what begins here is the consummation of modernity as regards the humanization of the human being in self-certain rationality—in a much more profound, that is, more encompassing and gripping way than in fascism. . . . The consummation required the decidedness of the historiological-technical in the sense of

the Complete "Mobilization" of all capacities of a humanity that has based itself upon itself. . . . (quoted in Polt, pp. 134–35)

In his *Black Notebooks* from the Third Reich and other contemporary posthumously published works like *Mindfulness* (*Besinnung*) and *The History of Beyng*, Heidegger systematically dismantles such National Socialist ideas as the people (*Volk*), nationalism, dictatorship, leadership, struggle (*Kampf*), cultural politics, *Lebensraum*, eugenics, and anti-intellectualism, connecting them all to nihilism, machination, brutality, and criminality. Thus, as Polt concludes, "It seems safe to say that by the late thirties, [Heidegger] was no Nazi anymore" (p. 153).

Surprisingly, though, even though Heidegger came to see National Socialism as an expression of nihilism rather than as an alternative to it, he still believed there were grounds to affirm it: "On the basis of the full insight into the earlier deception about the essence and historical essential force of National Socialism, there results the necessity of its affirmation, and indeed on *thoughtful* grounds" (quoted in Polt, p. 135).

Heidegger's rationale for this affirmation is a form of *accelerationism*. The clash of National Socialism vs. communism and liberal democracy may just be a family quarrel between different forms of technological nihilism, but the greater the conflict, the more likely the downfall of all forms of modernity, which would clear the ground for the emergence of a new inception. In Polt's words, "If being is essentially 'catastrophic' or 'tragic,' then we should not fear the collapse of modernity but accelerate it. Downfall can become a transition to the other inception" (p. 146). As Heidegger put it, "Before being can take place in its inceptive truth, being as the will must be broken, the world must be driven to implode, the earth driven to desolation, and man driven to mere labor. Only after this downfall, over a long time, the sudden while of the inception takes place" (quoted in Polt, p. 146).

Polt argues that even Heidegger's famous remark about the "inner truth and greatness" of National Socialism from his 1935 lecture course *Introduction to Metaphysics* has this accelerationist meaning. National Socialism is true and great because it has the potential to lead to the catastrophic downfall and self-over-coming of modernity (pp. 154–55). If so, this is a clear example of Heidegger using techniques of "esoteric" communication, since his private conception of "inner truth and greatness" is sharply different from what his audience would have taken him to mean.

So, although Heidegger stopped being a Nazi after 1934, he did not think that the alternatives of liberal democracy and communism were any better. Moreover, he still *supported* National Socialism because he still thought it would bring about the end of modernity. At first, he believed that it could actually inaugurate a new civilization. Later he believed that it could only destroy the existing order. But that was fine with him. Heidegger wanted the modern world to be destroyed. Which would imply that after the end of the Second World War, Heidegger's greatest regret was that Germany had been unable to drag her enemies down with her. It seems awfully cold. But Heidegger would probably have argued that modernity's survival dooms us to far greater horrors before it finally burns itself out.

Once one traverses Polt's scrupulous survey of Heidegger's remarks on political topics from the 1930s, it is legitimate to ask: In what sense was Heidegger a political philosopher? Heidegger brought phenomenology to bear on fundamental questions concerning metaphysics, epistemology, mind, language, technology, and the history of philosophy. His views on these matters are relevant to his own antimodernist and ethnonationalist political convictions, as well as to political philosophy in general. One can create a political philosophy on Heideggerian premises. But a political philosophy requires, at minimum, accounts of the basis of political legitimacy and the best political regime. If Heidegger himself worked out a political philosophy he never committed it to paper, at least in the nearly 100 volumes of his *Complete Edition* published so far. And Heidegger did not stint on paper.

It is tempting to parody Heidegger like Aristophanes mocks Socrates in the *Clouds*. Heidegger floats high above the political

realm in a basket, viewing everything through a long metaphysical spyglass, then declares apodictically that all political systems—liberal democratic, communist, and eventually even National Socialist—are "metaphysically identical." But couldn't this
identity be merely trivial, a matter of Heidegger's chosen perspective, thus as fallacious as concluding all cows are black because one views them at night?

Polt's concern is that "by dismissing all political and ethical
judgments in favor of metaphysical ones, Heidegger eliminates
any grounds for opposing totalitarianism" (p. 196). This is unfair
to Heidegger. First, claiming that all modern political ideologies
are *metaphysically* identical is not to say that they are all *morally*
the same. Just because Heidegger doesn't deal with the moral
dimensions of politics doesn't mean that others cannot. Second,
Heidegger's metaphysical identity thesis has predictive power.
Heidegger believed that all modern ideologies, regardless of
their differences, would ultimately converge into a totalitarian
dystopia because of their common underlying metaphysics.

What does it mean to say that communism, National Socialism, and liberal democracy are all metaphysically the same?
Heidegger understands metaphysics here to refer to the interpretation of man's relationship to the world.

First, all three systems presuppose a subject (the proletariat,
the race, the individual) that thinks of itself as *objective* and *sovereign*, i.e., uprooted from historical particularity and prejudice
and empowered to transform society in light of its imperatives.

Second, all three systems regard society as an object, as something that can be placed before the subject and transformed according to the subject's values and plans; this is what Heidegger
called "machination" (*Machenschaft*) in the thirties and "the essence of technology" after the war.

Third, these values and plans may vary, but they are all *intellectual constructs*, divorced from and at war with concrete traditions and ways of life. But if Heidegger is right that our practical
reason—our sense of measure, of limits, of the right thing in the
right place at the right time—is sustained by such rootedness,
then there is nothing to stop any modern ideology, liberal democracy included, from escalating into an increasingly totalitari-

an moral crusade against anything that resists it.

Heidegger's view of human nature is anti-totalitarian because it denies the deepest root of totalitarianism: the world-alienated and world-conquering subject. Instead, for Heidegger, subjectivity is embedded in traditional social practices. We are always part of society. We can't extract ourselves from it, then subject it totally to our plans. But neither are we in total thrall to these traditions, for they are ultimately practices for understanding and coping with what is *new*. The moment of application gives ample space for creativity. Moreover, it is both natural and noble to want to improve one's heritage before passing it on to the next generation.

Thus, although Heidegger never really worked out an account of the best regime, his account of man's relationship to history places him in the company of traditionalist conservatives like Edmund Burke, Michael Polanyi, and Michael Oakeshott, although Heidegger probably would have rejected the "classical liberal" elements of Polanyi and Oakeshott. Moreover, since subjectivity is embedded in a plurality of different languages and cultures, Heidegger's politics is inescapably ethnonationalist. Politics is always the expression of a particular people and the worldview and way of life that are second nature to it.

These views were present in *Being and Time*, so what explains Heidegger's turn toward National Socialism in 1930? Of course, Heidegger never embraced National Socialism because he thought it was a form of modern technological nihilism. That dawned on him later, after Hitler took power. But we can still ask what inclined Heidegger toward a *humanistic* historicism that made him receptive to the idea of great men engineering a fundamental change in history. The answer to that is: Nietzsche. According to Hans-Georg Gadamer, Heidegger stated that "Nietzsche ruined me,"[3] and it is important to note that Heidegger settled accounts with Nietzsche at the same time he broke with National Socialism. It is also important to note that Heidegger's subsequent anti-humanism represents a return to and intensifi-

---

[3] Hans-Georg Gadamer, "Heidegger und Nietzsche. Zu Nietzsche hat mich kaputtgemacht," *Aletheia* 9/10 (1996): 19.

cation of the ideas of *Being and Time*.

Polt's third chapter, "Recovering Politics," is a critique of Heidegger's political thought from a loosely "liberal democratic" perspective. I find it possible to share many of Polt's concerns without, however, embracing liberal democracy.

> Two decades into the twenty-first century, liberal democracy is under pressure from authoritarian, nationalist, and religious movements that are reacting nonphilosophically against trends that Heidegger scrutinized philosophically: an economic and cultural globalization that shows no respect for place and history; an anomie that cuts people off from their roots; the empty seductions of technology. These problems are real—but how do we address them without plunging into the tyranny and bloodshed unleashed by the anti-Enlightenment movements of the last century? Heidegger's reflections remain highly pertinent, but we must guard against abandoning the moral, political, and scientific ideals of the Enlightenment without articulating a responsible alternative. (p. 164).

I don't think Polt realizes how close his position is to the New Right as I define it. The project of the European New Right is to create a post-totalitarian European identity politics.

If one recognizes that "economic and cultural globalization that shows no respect for place and history; an anomie that cuts people off from their roots; the empty seductions of technology" are problems, you have already rejected the impetus of the entire modern political establishment.

If you wish to put boundaries on globalization, the most natural boundaries are nation states.[4] If you think place, history, and roots matter, then the best kind of state is the ethnostate.[5]

I have no quarrel with the Enlightenment's advocacy of the

---

[4] See Greg Johnson, "The End of Globalization," *Truth, Justice, & a Nice White Country* (San Francisco: Counter-Currents, 2015).

[5] See Greg Johnson, "The Ethnostate," *The White Nationalist Manifesto* (San Francisco: Counter-Currents, 2018).

mixed regime, religious tolerance, freedom of thought, and up-
holding reason and science as standards. Here the Enlightenment was merely trying to recover aspects of our classical heritage. The sovereign nation-state is another Enlightenment idea.

The only thing I really quarrel with is Polt blaming the cata-
clysms of the twentieth century on anti-Enlightenment thought.
Communism and liberal democracies have spilled oceans of
blood as well, because the twentieth century was a battleground
between different forms of technological nihilism. On this point,
Heidegger was correct.

Polt discusses three ways in which Heidegger's political
thought can be said to be irrationalist.

First, Heidegger rejects the idea that reason can emancipate
itself from its social and historical embeddedness. Polt's concern
is "whether a pluralistic public sphere is compatible with this
insight into our condition" (p. 169). But Heidegger does not reject reason as such, just a particular false conception of reason.
Heidegger would claim that reason, as the Enlightenment defines it, never actually existed. That doesn't mean that rational
deliberation about politics does not exist. It simply means that
we need a better account of how reason actually functions, even
though it is embedded within the context of social conventions
that it can never fully objectify and criticize.

Second, Polt is concerned that Heidegger's notion of the inception or event in which radical new meanings emerge and
take hold, including new standards of truth and goodness,
makes history ultimately unintelligible. But what makes this notion politically problematic is Heidegger's humanist twist that
certain human beings can impose a new inception, which places
them above all standards of truth and goodness. However, when
Heidegger rejected humanism, this would imply that all human
beings exist under obligation to some standards of truth and
goodness, although we might disagree about what they entail.

Third, Polt worries that Heidegger puts too much emphasis
on the idea of "emergency" (*Not*), for "a state of emergency is
typically invoked to authorize extraordinary powers and sus-
pend normal rights" (p. 163). Both in politics and in life in general, we can't lay down general rules that anticipate every con-

tingency. When we encounter something that the past has not equipped us for, individuals need to think and act anew. In his final chapter, Polt himself emphasizes how ubiquitous this experience is. Everyone has a sphere in which he is free to decide what to do when rules fail to decide for him. That goes for statesmen as well. This is a feature of every political system, however, although liberalism is deeply uncomfortable about this fact and tends to be in bad faith about it. But deciding without rules need not be unreason. Indeed, an insight into the good in particular circumstances is an essential trait of practical reason.

Polt recognizes that if Heidegger is right about human existence, all politics is inescapably identity politics. But identity politics is a complicated thing. Heidegger regards the identity of a people as a complex mix of race, language, culture, and history. Beyond that, he holds that the identity of a people is never finished and fixed but is instead an ongoing form of life that we should pass on to future generations better than we found it. Moreover, part of who we are is our future, which is in part a set of possibilities.

Polt then asks "if Heidegger understood national destiny as an open question, why did he go so wrong in politics?" (p. 170). Polt worries that Heidegger was "incapable of making any distinctions between a politics that might allow for the free exploration of selfhood and a politics that would shut the question down" (p. 170). He also remarks that "'Identity politics' at its crudest becomes a struggle for power among factions who wrestle against each other, but fail to wrestle with who they are" (p. 171).

Polt seems to think that because identity is a fluid and questionable phenomenon that we can have an identity politics of endlessly discussing and interpreting identity, and nothing else. This, of course, fits nicely with Carl Schmitt's (scathing) description of liberalism as attempting to turn politics into endless talk in order to avoid the necessity of decision and action. But politics cannot exclude action, so discussion must eventually be ended by decision.

But why should politics move from *discussing* identity to *shutting such discussion down*? Why should we move from wrestling with ourselves to wrestling with others? Sometimes, the decision is made for us. We might not choose to have enemies, but sometimes enemies choose us. Enmity arises, in particular, when peoples with different identities have to actually *live* in the same space under the same government. Polt recognizes this, again conceding quite a lot to the New Right, apparently without knowing it:

> A perfectly unified community is impossible. As Aristotle observes, an excess of unity destroys a *polis* as such, reducing it to a household or an organism (*Politics* 2.5). But of course, a community of people who have nothing in common would not be a community at all. Divisions can become so intense that a society breaks down in civil war. The question, then, is how much division, diversity, and dissent a community should tolerate, or even encourage.... Today, Muslim immigration into European countries has led to passionate debates about how much cultural diversity and change a country can stand before it ceases to be itself. (p. 172)

First, I should note that Aristotle is not talking about ethnic or racial diversity in the passage Polt cites. Instead, he is talking about whether property should be private or held in common.

Furthermore, it is *possible* for a polity to be—or to become—completely ethnically homogeneous, meaning an extended biological family sharing a common language, culture, and regime. The only question is whether or not such homogeneity is *desirable*. Polt clearly thinks diversity is desirable, but what is most important about this passage is that Polt concedes that diversity is not *unconditionally* good. There can be *too much* diversity, which leads to social conflict and breakdown. And what is the standard by which there can be too much diversity? Apparently, preserving the identity of a nation. Even this much political realism can lead to angry protests and witch hunts on college campuses today.

When diverse peoples stop *talking* about their identities and actually try to *live* together in the same system, there are tensions that can lead to violent conflict. The worst-case scenario is geno-cide, which Polt describes as the attempt to "settle the 'who' question in the worst possible way: by murdering those who 'we' are not" (p. 170). To avoid genocide, warring tribes need to separate, preferably into their own sovereign states. This is why the New Right advocates ethnonationalism. It is the best way to avoid needless hatred and violence between peoples and ensure their ability to live by their own lights without outside interfer-ence.

Polt also takes Heidegger to task for his lack of appreciation for negative freedom, including freedom of association and speech (pp. 181, 193). Heidegger, however, was not unthinking in his rejection of negative liberty. His critique was very much in the German idealist tradition of positive freedom. He empha-sized that freedom is only real if concretized in finite institutions:

> It is misguided to think one understands freedom most purely in its essence if one isolates it as a free-floating arbi-trariness. . . . The task is precisely the reverse, to conceive freedom in its finitude and to see that, by providing boundedness, one has neither impaired freedom nor cur-tailed its essence.[6]

The "free-floating arbitrariness" of negative freedom can be ab-ject slavery to one's base appetites if one chooses to be a drug addict. Your boss's freedom to fire you for your political opin-ions is your slavery to fear and want—and, as often as not, his slavery to public opinion. Conversely, if the state uses force to jail drug pushers and detox addicts, or to force employers to re-spect freedom of opinion, that increases freedom. Freedom be-comes unfreedom unless the state puts limits on it. One really can be "forced to be free."

Fortunately, one can make a Heideggerian and positive liber-tarian case for freedom of speech and assembly, based simply on the fact that since all leaders are finite and fallible beings, we

---

[6] Martin Heidegger, *The Metaphysical Foundations of Logic*, trans. Michael Heim (Bloomington: Indiana University Press, 1984), p. 196.

need the freedom to bring them bad news.[7]

Polt also chastises Heidegger for his failure to think about the common good of society and how we might determine it (pp. 60–67, 191). These are just criticisms. Heidegger's comments on the will of the leader, the will of the people, and how they might relate to the good in his 1933–1934 seminar *On the Essence and Concept of Nature, History, and State* are so rudimentary that they sound like they are literally occurring to him for the first time. They are the clearest indication that Heidegger really did not have a political philosophy.

But the idea of the common good is the best reason to reject liberal democracy. Liberal democracy tends to destabilize society by making false moral absolutes of freedom and equality. If freedom and equality are moral absolutes, then they must be taken to extremes, because no greater value can trump them. If freedom and equality are absolutes, then any negative consequences of absolutizing them just don't matter, and liberal democracy degenerates into cults immolating society to false idols. One can value freedom and equality. But one should put a higher value on the common good of society, which must trump freedom and equality whenever a conflict arises.

Time and Trauma is obligatory reading for Heidegger scholars and political theorists interested in Heidegger and the New Right. The strongest parts of the book are the first two chapters, which are largely expository. The weakest parts are the last two chapters, which are critical and reconstructive. Still, I am delighted that Polt chose to critique Heidegger and, by extension, to engage the New Right. I hope that in the future, though, the latter discussions will not be confined to the endnotes.

Counter-Currents, June 3, 2020

---

[7] Greg Johnson, "Freedom of Speech," *Toward a New Nationalism* (San Francisco: Counter-Currents, 2019).

RONALD BEINER'S
DANGEROUS MINDS

Ronald Beiner
Dangerous Minds: Nietzsche, Heidegger, and the Return of the Far Right
Philadelphia: University of Pennsylvania Press, 2018

Ronald Beiner is a Canadian Jewish political theorist who teaches at the University of Toronto. I've been reading his work since the early 1990s, starting with *What's the Matter with Liberalism?*[1] I have always admired Beiner's clear and lively writing and his ability to see straight through jargon and cant to hone in on the flaws of the positions he examines. He is also refreshingly free of Left-wing sectarianism and willing to engage with political theorists of the Right, like Leo Strauss, Eric Voegelin, Michael Oakeshott, and Hans-Georg Gadamer. Thus, although I was delighted that a theorist of his caliber had decided to write a book on the contemporary far Right, I was also worried that he might, after a typically open and searching engagement with our outlook, discover some fatal flaw.

But it turns out that an honest confrontation with our movement is a bridge too far. Beiner does not even wish to engage with our ideas, much less critique them. Instead, he uses the rise of the Right simply as lurid packaging to sell his publisher a book that focuses on Nietzsche and Heidegger. (The cover is of the torchlight march at Unite the Right, which is supposed to look sinister.)

Beiner's target is not the Right, but the Left, specifically those who think that Nietzsche and Heidegger can be profitably appropriated for Left-wing causes. To combat this view, he mounts a persuasive case that Nietzsche and Heidegger are deeply anti-liberal thinkers. Thus, although *Dangerous Minds* is sensationalist

---

[1] Ronald Beiner, *What's the Matter with Liberalism?* (Berkeley: University of California Press, 1992).

and dismissive in its treatment of our movement, it is nevertheless extremely useful to us. If anyone wants to understand why Nietzsche and Heidegger are so useful to the New Right, Beiner gives a clear and engaging account in a bit more than 100 pages.

Since Beiner wants to cast our movement in the worst possible light, he naturally begins with Hailgate:

> In the fateful fall of 2016, a far-right ideologue named Richard B. Spencer stirred up some fame for himself by exclaiming in a conference packed with his followers not far from the White House: "Hail Trump! Hail our people! Hail victory!" On the face of it, this mad proclamation would appear to have nothing in common with the glorious tradition of Western philosophy. (p. 1)

But think again.

Beiner then quotes Spencer denouncing "fucking middle class" values and proclaiming "I love empire, I love power, I love achievement." We even learn from a Jewish female reporter that Spencer will sometimes "get a boner" from reading about Napoleon. (Another triumph of press engagement.)

This is Nietzsche's work, declares Beiner.

Beiner goes on to call Spencer a "lunatic ideologue" (p. 11) and an advocate of "virulently antiliberal, antidemocratic radicalism" (p. 12). He blames it all on a graduate seminar on Nietzsche that Spencer took at the University of Chicago. This is laying it on a bit thick, since Spencer is not offering a system of ideas. He's just dropping Nietzsche's name to impress middlebrow journalists. Perhaps sensing this, Beiner turns his attention to a prolific author of essays and books, Alexander Dugin. Beiner easily establishes the Nietzschean and Heideggerian pedigree of Dugin's dangerous ideas.

Naturally, at this point, I was wondering if I was next, so I flipped to the back of the book to see if my name appeared in the index. But there is no index. (This from a serious academic publisher?) So I continued to read. By the end, I was a bit relieved, and maybe a bit miffed, to receive no mention at all in *Dangerous Minds*. Nor is *Counter-Currents* mentioned by name, although it is referred to on page 12 as "One of the typically odious far-right websites" and on page 150 as "Another far-right outfit of the same ilk" as Arktos. In the first case, Beiner refers to James O'Meara's review of Jason Jorjani's *Prometheus and Atlas*, but he does not name O'Meara or give the URL of the review.[2] (Jorjani is, however, singled out for abuse as a "crackpot philosopher.") In the second case, Beiner provides the URL of my Heidegger commemoration but does not cite the author or title.[3] Beiner is known as a Left-wing admirer of Leo Strauss and Allan Bloom. These glaring oversights might lead those of a Straussian bent to think that Beiner regards *Counter-Currents*, James O'Meara, me, and perhaps Collin Cleary,[4] who is also noticeably omitted, to be of central importance. But of course he has plausible deniability.

Beiner zeroes in on equality as the essential issue that divides the Left and the Right:

> A view of society where all individuals are fundamentally equal or a view of society where people can live meaningful lives only under the banner of fundamental hierarchy: this is an either/or, not a moral-political choice that can be submitted to compromise or splitting the difference. . . . [O]ne either sees egalitarianism as essential to the proper acknowledgement of universal human dignity, or one sees it as the destruction of what's most human because it's incompatible with human nobility rightly understood. (p. 8)

This is basically correct, but I have two caveats.

First, I think equality and liberty are genuine political values. But they are not the most important values. Individual self-actualization and the pursuit of the common good are more important than individual liberty, for instance. And justice is more

---

[2] James J. O'Meara, "Jason Jorjani's *Prometheus & Atlas*," *Counter-Currents*, September 26, 2016.

[3] Greg Johnson, "Remembering Martin Heidegger: September 30, 1889–May 26, 1976," *Counter-Currents*, September 30, 2017.

[4] Collin Cleary, "Heidegger: An Introduction for Anti-Modernists," Parts 1–4, *Counter-Currents*, June 4–7, 2012.

important than equality, since justice requires unequal people receive unequal treatment. But even here, justice demands that unequal status and rewards be *proportionate* to unequal merit. By this Aristotelian view of justice, however, most forms of contemporary social and political inequality are grossly unjust.

This is why I oppose people on the Right who praise "hierarchy" as such. Not all hierarchies are just. Thus one can defend the principle of hierarchy without embracing ideas like hereditary monarchy, aristocracy, and caste, much less slavery. These are at best merely imperfect historical illustrations of the principle of hierarchy, not blueprints for the future.

Second, the notion of "universal human dignity" is simply an article of faith, like Stoic and Christian ideas of providence and liberal ideas of progress. Progress and providence are our trump cards against ultimate misfortune. They allow us to keep believing that things will work out in the end. "Dignity" is really a trump card against dehumanization: It is the assertion that no matter how botched, degraded, and corrupt a human being is, he is still a human being; he still possesses some intrinsic worth that he can use, as a measure of last resort, to gain some consideration from the rest of us. But when aliens land and discover that human beings are delicious, appeals to the universal dignity of rational beings are not going to save us. True nobility requires that we face reality and dispense with such moralistic illusions.

But that does not mean that we dispense with empathy for others. I have zero patience for people on the Right who defend slavery, colonialism, imperialism, and genocide. They are guilty of another form of providential wishful thinking, for they apparently feel themselves invulnerable to the sufferings they would cheerfully inflict on others. It does not occur to them that others could do the same to them. But nobility requires thinking and living without such illusions. You might be high and mighty today, but you are not bulletproof (which is really all Hobbes meant by equality). Empathy allows us to imagine ourselves in the positions of others. Fortune can elevate or lower us into the positions of others. And if none of us are immune to fortune, *then we should create a political system in which we could morally bear to trade places with anyone,* a society in which all social stations are fundamentally just. This leads to the sort of live-and-let-live ethos that is at the core of ethnonationalism as I define it.

This is why I don't regard Alexander Dugin and Richard Spencer as contributing anything to White Nationalism, which is the advocacy of ethnic self-determination for all white peoples. Instead, they are simply apologists for Russian imperial revanchism. Spencer regards ethnonationalism as "petty," siding with the UK against Scottish independence, the EU against Brexit, and Spain against Catalan independence. But although he opposes the UK leaving the EU, he opposes Ukraine joining it. He praises the EU as a transnational, imperial organization—but not NATO. Clearly, he is more interested in shilling for Russian geopolitical interests than in setting forth a coherent moral and political framework for white survival. I can't blame Beiner for focusing on Dugin and Spencer, however, because they embrace all of Nietzsche's most lurid and questionable ideas as well as his good ones.

BEINER ON NIETZSCHE

According to Beiner's chapter on "Reading Nietzsche in an Age of Resurgent Fascism," the "one central, animating Nietzschean idea" is: "Western civilization is going down the toilet because of too much emphasis on truth and rationality and too much emphasis on equal human dignity" (p. 24). This passage also illustrates the vulgar and often hysterical tone of Beiner's polemic. *Dangerous Minds* has a rambling, informal, often autobiographical style that makes it read like an extended blog post. Beiner also peppers his prose with exclamation points, sometimes four or five to the page, to drive his points home. I began to worry that he would soon resort to emoticons.

Nietzsche offers two arguments against liberalism. First, liberalism destroys the meaning of life. Second, liberalism destroys human nobility.

For Nietzsche, a meaningful life requires a normative culture as the context or "horizon" in which each individual is immersed and formed. In short, a meaningful life is rooted in ethnic identity, although Nietzsche does not put it in these terms, as he was deeply alienated from and ambivalent about his own

German identity. A normative culture provides an encompassing worldview and a hierarchy of values. These need not be
"true" in any metaphysical sense in order to provide foundations for a meaningful life, hence the danger of modernity's high
valuation of truth and rationality. These horizons are always
plural (there are many different cultures), and they are *closed*
(they generate differences between insiders and outsiders, us
and them; thus they are "political" in Carl Schmitt's sense of the
word).

Liberalism destroys meaning because it is cosmopolitan and
egalitarian. Its cosmopolitanism opens horizons to other cultures
and undermines attachment to one's own culture. Its egalitarian-
ism overthrows value hierarchies that make people feel bad
about themselves. The result is the collapse of rootedness and
meaning and the emergence of nihilism. This is why Nietzsche
"regards old-fashioned nineteenth-century liberalism—to say
nothing of radicalized twentieth- and twenty-first century versions—as rendering culture *per se* impossible" (p. 34).

Beiner doesn't offer a very clear account of why Nietzsche
thinks liberalism undermines human nobility. The short answer
is that it is simply the political application of the slave revolt in
morals, in which the aristocratic virtues of the ancients were
transmuted into Christian and eventually liberal vices, and the
vices of the enslaved and downtrodden were transmuted into
virtues.

But what makes us noble in the first place? Like Hegel, Nietzsche believes that human nobility shows itself by triumphing
over the fear of death and loss and doing beautiful and good
things in spite of them. Thus, human nobility is essentially connected with facing up to the tragic character of human life and
finding the strength to carry on.

Liberalism, like Platonism, Stoicism, and Christianity, is anti-
tragic because it is based on faith in providence, the idea that the
universe is ruled by and directed toward the good—appearances
to the contrary notwithstanding. Providence denies the ultimate
reality of loss, finitude, and evil, blinding us to the tragic dimension of life and replacing it with the stoner mantra that "It's all
good." It is a delusion of ultimate metaphysical invulnerability

to evil and loss.

Modern liberals replace faith in providence with faith in progress, which they believe will result in the perfection of mankind and the amelioration of human suffering and evils. It is a false vision of the world that smothers the possibility of human nobility. Although Beiner has the *chutzpah* to suggest that maybe Nietzscheans can ennoble themselves by enduring life in the "iron cage" of modernity and learning to love the Last Man (p. 116). (Why not ennoble oneself even more by living with head-lice as well?)

The plurality of horizons also means the possibility of existential conflict and the necessity of choosing and taking responsibility for one's choices. As Schmitt argued, however, the whole liberal ethos is to replace the government of responsible choosers — the sovereign — with the government of laws, rules, and anonymous bureaucrats.

Beiner doesn't delve too deeply into Nietzsche's views of nobility because he wants to dismiss them based on Nietzsche's praise of slavery, caste, war, and cruelty, which did accompany the emergence of aristocratic values. Furthermore, the leisure that gave rise to science and high culture was secured by the labor of slaves.

However, one can legitimately ask if we need to become barbarians again to bring about a rebirth of aristocratic values and high culture. For instance, the advocates of Social Credit — the preferred economic theory of interwar Anglophone fascists — envisioned a world in which nobility and creativity are unleashed once machines relieve us all of the necessity of work.[5]

But if we cannot renew civilization without starting over from scratch, then I would gladly hit the reset button rather than allow the world to decline endlessly into detritus. Thus, on Nietzschean and Heideggerian grounds, it makes sense to try to renew the world, because if one fails, that failure might contribute to the civilizational reset that we need. Indeed, the more cata-

---

[5] See Greg Johnson, "Money for Nothing," *Counter-Currents*, January 17, 2012; reprinted in *Truth, Justice, & a Nice White Country* (San Francisco: Counter-Currents, 2015).

strophic the failure, the greater the chance of a fresh start. The only way we can't win is if we don't try.

BEINER ON HEIDEGGER

Beiner's chapter on "Reading Heidegger in an Age of Resurgent Fascism" is less incisive than his account of Nietzsche, largely because he does not see how close Heidegger really is to Nietzsche. Beiner takes Heidegger's question of Being at face value and finds it rather bizarre that Heidegger could think that modern civilization is going to hell because of forgetting about Being. But for Heidegger, Being = meaning, and the modern oblivion of Being is basically what Nietzsche meant by the collapse of closed normative horizons and the rise of nihilism. Indeed, Heidegger's concept of *Dasein* simply refers to man as a being situated within and defined by horizons of meaning. The occlusion of these horizons by the false individualism and cosmopolitanism of modernity leads to nihilism, a life deprived of meaning.

Heidegger thought National Socialism could bring about the spiritual renewal of the German people—and presumably any other nation that tried it—by rejecting cosmopolitanism and individualism and reaffirming the rootedness, community, and the closed horizon of the nation. He rejected National Socialism when he came to see it as just another form of modern technological nihilism. Nietzsche, of course, rejected German nationalism, but Heidegger's thinking was truer to the implications of Nietzsche's thinking about the closed cultural horizons that grant meaning.

Beiner is at his best in his reading of Heidegger's "Letter on Humanism," his post-war statement publicly inaugurating "the late Heidegger." Beiner correctly discerns that Heidegger's lament against the "homelessness" of modern man and his loss of *Heimat* (homeland) is an expression of the same fundamentally reactionary, anti-modern, anti-cosmopolitan, and pro-nationalist sentiments that led him to embrace National Socialism. Indeed, there's good reason to think that Heidegger never changed his fundamental political philosophy at all. The only thing that changed was his evaluation of National Socialism and his adoption of a more oblique and esoteric way of speaking about politics under the repressive conditions of the Occupation and the Federal Republic. Carrying out Heidegger's project of offering a case for a non-nihilistic, non-totalitarian form of ethnonationalism is the project of the New Right as I define it.

HEIDEGGER & THE HOLOCAUST

Beiner, like many Jewish commentators, seems to feel that Heidegger owes him a personal apology for the Holocaust. We are told that Heidegger's silence about the Holocaust is unforgivable. But when we point out that Heidegger did say something about the Holocaust, namely that it was a sinister application of mechanized modern mass slaughter to human beings, we are told that this view is also unforgivable, since the Holocaust somehow transcends all attempts to classify and understand it. Which would seem to require that we say nothing about it at all, but we have already learned that this is unforgivable as well.

Beiner tells the story of Rudolf Bultmann's visit to Heidegger after the war, when he told Heidegger, "Now you must like Augustine write your retractions [*Retractiones*] . . . in the final analysis for the truth of your thought." Bultmann continues: "Heidegger's face became a stony mask. He left without saying anything further" (p. 119).

Beiner treats this as outrageous. But Heidegger's reaction is not hard to understand. He had nothing to retract. He felt that he had done nothing wrong. He was not responsible for the war or the Holocaust. They were none of his doing or his intention. They were part and parcel of the very nihilism that he opposed. The fact that the National Socialist regime went so terribly wrong did not refute Heidegger's basic diagnosis of the problems of modern rootlessness and nihilism but rather proved how all-pervasive they were. Nor did anything the Nazis did refute the deep truth of ethnonationalism as the political corollary of spiritually awakening from the nightmare of liberal modernity. Thus Heidegger absolutely refused to say anything about the war or the Holocaust that could be interpreted as conceding that modern liberal democracy had somehow been proven true. Instead, he continued to make essentially the same arguments as he made before the war, but in more esoteric terms by focusing on rootlessness and technology.

Bultmann was telling Heidegger to lie, to retract beliefs he believed were true, and to do it in the name of "the truth of [his] thought" when in fact the only motive could be to win the approval of the victors. But that approval was something Heidegger decided to do without. Frankly, Bultmann was making an indecent proposal, and Heidegger's stony silence was admirably restrained.

Beiner mentions that according to Gadamer, Heidegger "was so preoccupied by modernity's forgetfulness of Being [rootlessness, nihilism] that even the Nazi genocide 'appeared to him as something minimal compared to the future that awaits us'" (p. 107). Here's another unforgivable statement breaching Heidegger's unforgivable silence. But this unforgivable statement is, unfortunately, quite prophetic. For the consummation of global technological civilization, including the erasure of borders and the destruction of roots, will lead to a genocide far vaster and more complete than the Holocaust. I refer the reader to my chapters "White Extinction" and "White Genocide" in *The White Nationalist Manifesto* and especially my essay "Why the Holocaust Happened, and Why It Won't Happen Again" in *Toward a New Nationalism.*[6]

A NEW AGE OF GODS?

Both Nietzsche and Heidegger think that spiritual health requires *unreflective belief in and commitment to* a closed, normatively binding cultural horizon. Christianity, post-Socratic philosophy, and the Enlightenment, however, made self-reflection and universal truth into transcendent values. But as Nietzsche argued, this was a self-defeating move, for Christianity could not stand up to rational criticism. Reason soon escaped the control of the Church, which led to the downfall of Christianity (Nietzsche's "death of God"), the erasure of the West's horizon, and

---

[6] Greg Johnson, *The White Nationalist Manifesto* (San Francisco: Counter-Currents, 2018). Greg Johnson, *Toward a New Nationalism* (San Francisco: Counter-Currents, 2019).

the rise of modern nihilism. It follows that the return to spiritual health requires the emergence of a new age of unreflective belief and commitment. Giambattista Vico called this an "Age of Gods," the first age of a new historical cycle.

The great question is: Can a new "Age of Gods" emerge within the context of our present civilization, or must the modern world perish utterly—completely liquidating the Western tradition of philosophy, science, and liberalism—so that mankind can truly *believe, belong,* and *obey* again? The new horizons and myths that we need, moreover, cannot be "chosen," for adopting a belief system as a matter of choice is not an alternative to nihilism, it is just an expression of it. Genuine belief is not chosen. It chooses you. It does not belong to you. You belong to it.

Nietzsche believed that a new age of gods could be imposed by great philosopher-legislators who could create new myths and new tables of values. Under Nietzsche's sway, Heidegger believed this as well, and it accounts for why he thought National Socialism could lead to a spiritual renewal of Germany. It was only later that Heidegger realized that National Socialism was not an alternative to nihilism but an expression of it.

It was at this point that Heidegger began his great confrontation with Nietzsche in the mid-1930s. According to Gadamer, Heidegger once said "Nietzsche ruined me."[7] I think Nietzsche ruined Heidegger by offering him nihilism as a cure for nihilism. Nietzsche made Heidegger a Nazi. Heidegger overcame Nazism by overcoming Nietzsche.

In Heidegger's later terminology, Nietzsche and National Socialism were both "humanistic," premised on the idea that the human mind creates culture, whereas in fact culture creates the human mind. No genuine belief can be chosen. It has to seize us. This is one of the senses of Heidegger's later concept of *Ereignis,* often translated "the event of appropriation": The beginning of a new historical epoch seizes and enthralls us. This is the meaning of Heidegger's later claim that "Only a god can save us now"—as opposed to a philosopher-dictator.

---

[7] Hans-Georg Gadamer, "Heidegger und Nietzsche. Zu Nietzsche hat mich kaputtgemacht," *Aletheia* 9/10 (1996): 19.

One could, however, read Nietzsche in a non-humanistic way, if one sees his rhapsodies about the *Übermensch*, the philosopher-legislator, and the coming century of global wars (yes, Nietzsche predicted that) not as a solution to modern nihilism, but as a way of intensifying it to the breaking point to accelerate the downfall of the modern world and inaugurate a new age of gods. ("That which is falling should also be pushed.") If this is Nietzsche's true view, then offering nihilism to cure nihilism is not a self-contradiction, it is just sound homeopathic medicine.

Beiner asks "are any of us really prepared to entertain the possibility of the comprehensive cancelling-out of modernity to which Heidegger in his radicalism seems committed?" (p. 105). Elsewhere he asks ". . . with what do we undertake to replace [liberal modernity]? A regime of warriors and priests? A return from Enlightenment to magic?" (p. 132). But Beiner is asking these questions from within liberal modernity, and of course from within that perspective, people are going to cling to liberalism simply out of fear. From Heidegger's point of view, we will only have a solution when individuals can no longer pose such questions. Instead, the answers will be imposed upon us by historical forces outside our comprehension or control.

A Smug Criticism of Smugness

Beiner's conclusion, "How to Do Theory in Politically Treacherous Times," is, like the rest of his book, directed to Leftist academics. He makes a strong case against the smugness and complacency of contemporary political theorists, who think they can ignore the Right because we have been refuted by history: "For Rawls, Rorty, and Habermas, Nietzsche has been refuted by history and sociology. He hasn't! He can only be refuted by a more compelling account of the human good" (p. 125). This is excellent advice, but it ill-accords with Beiner's own supremely smug, question-begging, and dismissive tone throughout *Dangerous Minds*. Judging from what he does, as opposed to what he says, Beiner's real aim is not to intellectually engage the Right, but to censor and suppress it. But if Beiner really does want to debate the philosophical foundations of the New Right, I'm game.

SHOULD WE READ HEIDEGGER & NIETZSCHE?

If Nietzsche and Heidegger are so dangerous to liberal democracy, shouldn't something be *done* to keep their books out of the hands of impressionable young men?

Beiner ends his discussion of Nietzsche by referring to Leo Strauss's advice to Canadian conservative political philosopher George Grant, who was about to embark on a series of popular radio lectures on Nietzsche. Strauss viewed Nietzsche as a profoundly dangerous thinker and advised Grant not to talk about Nietzsche at all but simply refer to his "epigones" Freud and Weber. The only reason Beiner brings this up, of course, is to plant the idea that academics should drop Nietzsche from the canon. Beiner, however, strenuously denies that this is his intent in his Introduction:

> Hopefully no reader of my book will draw from it the unfortunate conclusion that we should just walk away from Nietzsche and Heidegger — that is, stop reading them. [Of course reading them does not necessarily entail teaching them, especially to undergraduates.] On the contrary, I think that we need to read them in ways that make us more conscious of, more reflective about, and more self-critical of the limits of the liberal view of life and hence what defines that view of life. But if one is handling intellectually radioactive materials, one has to be much less naïve about what one is dealing with. . . . We need to open our eyes, at once *intellectually*, *morally*, and *politically*, to just how dangerous they are. (p. 14)

But this seems disingenuous in light of Beiner's repeated assertion that Nietzsche and Heidegger should have censored their own ideas insofar as they are dangerous to liberal modernity:

> There is a kind of insane recklessness to Nietzsche — as if nothing he could write, no matter how irresponsible, no matter how inflammatory, could possibly do any harm. All that matters is *raising the stakes*, and there is no such

thing as raising the stakes *too high*. (p. 63)

One has to ask: "To whom does Beiner think Nietzsche is being irresponsible? What could his thought possibly harm?" The answer, of course, is the modern liberal democratic world, the world that Nietzsche rejects, the world that *Nietzsche crafted his doctrines to destroy*.

Beiner is even more blatant in his advocacy of self-censorship in Heidegger's case:

> Near the end of his life, Heidegger decided to include the *Black Notebooks* (including explicitly racist passages conjuring up a diabolical conspiracy on the part of "World Judaism" [sic: World Jewry]) in the official *Collected Works*, whereas any reasonably sane person would have burned them, or at least burned the most incriminating passages. It's as if he either were trying to spur a revival of fascist ideology or intended to confess to the world just how grievously stained he had been by that ideology. All of this is thoroughly damning. (pp. 113–14)

Again, one must ask: "Sane by whose standards? Incriminating to whom? Damning by whose standards?" The answer, of course, is: modern liberal democrats. But Heidegger thought these people were intellectually benighted and morally corrupt. So why should he censor his thought to conform to their sensibilities? To hell with them. He was addressing himself to freer minds, to a better world, to generations yet to come.

At the beginning of his Heidegger chapter, Beiner also writes:

> The question I'm raising in this chapter is whether, finding ourselves now in a political landscape where the possibility increasingly looms of Heidegger as a potential resource for the far right, it might be best for left Heideggerianism (a paradox to begin with) to close up shop. (p. 67)

Since virtually everyone teaching Heidegger in academia today is a Leftist, this basically amounts to removing Heidegger from the canon. Beiner's talk of looming possibilities and potential resources is off the mark, for Heidegger already is a resource and inspiration for the New Right, and he knows this. (Frankly, I hope Left-wing Heideggerians close up shop soon. It would be an ideal opportunity to launch the Heidegger Graduate School.[8])

It is absurd to wish that Nietzsche and Heidegger had censored their ideas to remove their challenges to the system they despised and wished to destroy. If liberals want to stop these ideas from influencing policy, they need to refute them. Demanding censorship is simply an admission that one cannot refute ideas rationally and thus must repress them. Asking one's opponents to engage in self-censorship takes some brass. If liberals can't refute anti-liberals like Nietzsche and Heidegger, they are just going to have to screw up their resolve and do their own dirty work. This is hardly a stretch, sadly, since the suppression of dissent is second nature to modern academics. It's really all they have left.

Indeed, if wishing aloud that Nietzsche and Heidegger had censored themselves has any practical meaning today, it is as a suggestion that political theorists and philosophers censor themselves and their syllabi, i.e., remove Nietzsche and Heidegger from the canon.

If Beiner is really arguing that Leftists should stop teaching Nietzsche and Heidegger, he apparently did not anticipate what would happen if his book fell into the hands of Rightist readers like me. For *Dangerous Minds*, despite its obnoxious rhetoric and smug dismissal of our movement, is a very helpful introduction to Nietzsche and Heidegger as anti-liberal thinkers. Thus I recommend it highly. And if I have anything to say about it, this book will help create a whole lot more dangerous minds, a whole new generation of Right-wing Nietzscheans and Heideggerians.

Counter-Currents, April 23, 2018

---

[8] See "Graduate School with Heidegger," below.

DUGIN ON HEIDEGGER

Alexander Dugin
Martin Heidegger: The Philosophy of Another Beginning
Edited and translated by Nina Kouprianova
Preface by Paul E. Gottfried
Whitefish, Mt.: Radix, 2014

Martin Heidegger is one of the most influential philosophers of the twentieth century. So it should come as no surprise that Heidegger, a life-long man of the Right, is also an important thinker for the New Right in Europe and North America.

Heidegger belonged to the broad German Conservative Revolutionary intellectual current. He fell in and out with the National Socialist movement. His encounter with National Socialism and his post-War thinking on modernity, technology, and the possibility of a new dispensation are of enduring relevance to the New Right project of defining a post-totalitarian alternative to both the Old Right and the existing Jewish/Leftist hegemony.

Thus a book-length discussion of Heidegger by Alexander Dugin, who is loosely affiliated with the European New Right, would seem a welcome contribution. There would be two reasons to read Dugin's book on Heidegger: first, for what it reveals about Heidegger; second, for what it reveals about Dugin. Unfortunately, after nearly 400 pages, I felt that I had learned very little about either thinker.

It isn't easy to write a book about Heidegger, who is notoriously obscure. Unfortunately, Dugin's method of exposition leans heavily on paraphrase and repetition, and if you have trouble reading Heidegger himself, Dugin's restatement will hardly be more intelligible. If you are just looking for an exposition of Heidegger in English, there are many better choices, for example, Graham Harman's *Heidegger Explained*,[1] which is lucid,

---

[1] Graham Harman, *Heidegger Explained: From Phenomenon to Thing* (Chicago: Open Court, 2007).

comprehensive, and concise at around 180 pages.

I also hoped that this volume would throw light on why Dugin proposes Heidegger's concept of *Dasein* as the "subject" of what he calls the "fourth political theory." Unfortunately, it adds nothing to what Dugin has said on the matter in *The Fourth Political Theory*.

Heidegger's favorite word is "Being" (*Sein*), which he uses constantly but defines only infrequently, incompletely, and in passing. This makes it tempting for readers to plug in notions of Being inherited from the history of philosophy: God, objective reality, ultimate reality, what all beings have in common, etc. All these interpretations founder, however, on the fact that Heidegger insists that *Being somehow requires man*, or human being (*Dasein*).

Heidegger does not, however, mean that nothing existed before mankind evolved, or that the universe was completed by the evolution of man. For Heidegger, Being does not mean *beings* (objectively existing things). Nor does Being mean "ultimate reality" (the One, Brahman, God, etc.). Nor does it mean something all beings have in common, like a common element or particle, or the widest, emptiest category.

For Heidegger, *Being = meaning*. To be is to be meaningful. Meaningful to whom? Meaningful to man. And insofar as man is a being who has meaning, Heidegger refers to man as *Dasein* (or *Da-Sein*, the place of Being).

Meaningful things do not, however, exist in isolation. They are parts of a larger context of meaning, which Heidegger calls a "world." Again, the tendency is to think of a world as an assemblage of objectively existing beings, which does not require man. Surely it makes sense to speak of the "world of the dinosaurs," even though mankind did not exist at the time. Heidegger does not deny that dinosaurs existed before us, or that they existed in a web of relationships (an ecosystem). But, again, Heidegger is using "world" in a specific way to mean "world of meaning," which *requires* man (*Dasein*) as the one *to whom* things are meaningful.

But Heidegger's ultimate topic is not Being (meaning) but *the meaning of Being* (the meaning of meaning). This is the question of *what makes meaning possible.*

Since Being always involves man, the question of the meaning of Being involves man as well. Man and Being have a relationship of mutual belonging. Heidegger's term for this relationship is *Ereignis*, which ordinarily means "event" but for him also means (1) *taking hold* (*Er-eignis*, usually translated as appropriation or "enowning") and (2) *beholding* (*Er-äugnis*, be-eyeing).

An English word that captures both taking hold and beholding is "enthrallment." To enthrall literally means to enslave, but also it means to captivate or enchant by a spectacle. Being and man are mutually in thrall, mutually enthralled. "Enthrallment" also captures Heidegger's insistence that individuals do not construct their own worlds of meaning, but are taken up and thrown into pre-existing worlds of meaning by greater historical forces: languages, cultures, traditions. Meaning comes in worlds, and worlds are collective, not individual. And collective meanings seize and hold sway over individuals.

In *Being and Time*, Heidegger began his account of meaning and its relationship to man using the subject-centered phenomenological method adopted from his teacher Edmund Husserl. But the collective nature of meaning, and the fact that the individual has collective meanings imposed upon him, chafed against the phenomenological method, in which the philosopher reflects upon how the world is given to him/us. Because Heidegger realized that the human subject itself is structured by inherited meanings (language, culture, tradition), he needed to move outside the subject-centered phenomenological perspective and explore the relationship of man and meaning from the side of meaning rather then the side of man.

Being and Time remained unfinished because, at the time, Heidegger was unable to articulate this shift in perspective. Heidegger characterized his later philosophy not as transcendental phenomenology but as "*seinsgeschichtliches Denken*," which is literally and misleadingly translated as "Being-historical thinking." Heidegger, however, is not thinking of mere history, but of what lies above and behind history, the intellectual conditions that make it possible. For Heidegger, history is not just a record of rulers, battles, and inventions, but of the underlying assumptions about reality that shape politics, warfare, and technology.

Ordinarily, the German *Geschichte* means "history." But Heidegger is attentive to the roots and etymological associations of *Geschichte*, namely *schicken* (to send) and *Geschick* (destiny). A good English equivalent is "dispensation," since it has the sense of a received order, the existing regime. Furthermore, a dispensation is always finite, time-bound, epochal. One speaks of "the present dispensation," because one is aware of past and future ones. Since for Heidegger Being = meaning, "Being-historical thinking" really means "thinking about the dispensations of meaning."

Heidegger divides European history into a succession of different epochs or dispensations of meaning: the pre-Socratic and Socratic periods of classical thought, the Christian world, early modernity, and the completion of modernity in modern nihilism, i.e., man-centered technological materialism.

For Heidegger, the history of Western philosophy, from Plato to Nietzsche, is a trajectory of decline. The objective reality of beings is forgotten, as Being is defined in terms of knowability in thought and manipulability in action. The intimate connection of man and world is forgotten, replaced with the dualism of mind and matter. The dependence of the individual on received systems of collective meaning is forgotten, replaced with arrant individualism and the idea that human history and human nature can be mastered and reconstructed according to conscious plans. Finally, we have forgotten the fact that none of this was inevitable, that another dispensation—the new beginning of Dugin's title—is possible.

And Heidegger makes quite clear that a new beginning is highly desirable, for he rejects modernity—and the Western philosophical tradition that gives rise to it—in the strongest possible terms as leading to the dehumanization of man and the destruction of nature by establishing the dominion of an anthropocentric, technological materialism, which encompasses both communism and liberal capitalism. (Heidegger had no objection to technology *per se*, but to technology linked to a leveling materialism and man-centered values.)

In his memoir *Philosophical Apprenticeships*, Hans-Georg Gadamer, one of Heidegger's most eminent students, recounted a meeting after the First World War in which different radical ideas for the salvation of Germany were proposed. One voice declared that *phenomenology* was the only possible solution.[2] Heidegger himself certainly linked phenomenology to the crisis of his time, thus his philosophical writings have an intensely rhetorical dimension that is by turns moral, political, religious, poetic, prophetic, eschatological, and often strongly nationalistic.

Heidegger hoped that National Socialism would provide a fundamental alternative to modern man-centered materialism, but when National Socialism itself turned out to be another form of materialist modernity, Heidegger criticized it from the Right and never gave up the hope that a real Right-wing alternative would emerge. Creating that alternative is the aim of New Right today.

After the Second World War, Heidegger gave up on politics proper. If the problem with the modern world is the idea that we can understand and control everything, including history and society, then working out and implementing an anti-modernist political program is not a solution, but just another version of the problem.

The only way to overturn the idea that everything can be understood and controlled is to find things that are mysterious and uncontrollable. For Heidegger, the *source* of the idea that everything can be understood and controlled can itself be neither understood nor controlled. When one looks into a light, the light itself obscures its source. The same is true of meaning. The modern dispensation of meaning, like all dispensations of meaning, arises from sources that are obscure. This is why Heidegger speaks of each dispensation as an *Ereignis*, an event, meaning an inscrutable contingency.

For Heidegger, meaning is finite: If the intelligibility and manipulability of beings is highlighted by the modern dispensation,

[2] Hans-Georg Gadamer, *Philosophical Apprenticeships*, trans. Robert R. Sullivan (Cambridge: MIT Press, 1985), p. 15.

that simply means that other dimensions are being obscured. And the source of that dispensation is itself obscure. But if the modern dispensation is finite, it can never be final. A new dispensation can dawn. What is hidden can come to light, and what is illuminated can become obscure. We do not know how or why.

But we do know that man and meaning belong together.

That means that the present dispensation cannot exist without us. Even though it holds us in thrall, it somehow depends upon us as well. We sustain it whenever we act under the assumption that everything can be transparent and available. Whenever we want things to be faster or cheaper or more convenient, we are sustaining the modern dispensation.

But what if we attune ourselves to the mysterious and uncontrollable? What if we cultivate a taste for the poetic and the mystical? What if we reject utilitarian values for the beautiful, the useless, or the heroic? What if we prize uniqueness over uniformity, the earthy over the plastic, slow food over fast food, the limits of nature over the power of the technologically weaponized will? What if we opt out of mainstream culture and create a counter-culture that cultivates a different worldview and way of life? Then we are no longer sustaining the present dispensation. And if enough of us opt out, surely a new dispensation must dawn. We know not how or why.

But we do know that historical change is possible.

Indeed, we know that it is already happening. Heidegger did not believe that philosophers or poets are the hidden legislators of mankind, excogitating theories that give rise to new historical dispensations. This is pure anthropocentrism, the idea that man makes history rather than history makes man. Instead, Heidegger believed that philosophers and poets *receive* their ideas from the hidden currents of the *Zeitgeist*. They only look like they create ideas because they receive them first.

Thus Heidegger's own thought, and the thought of others like him, is not to be dismissed as merely subjective and ineffectual ideas hatched by alienated dreamers. For Heidegger sees the *very existence* of such ideas as the stirring of the most sensitive souls, the earliest risers, to the dawn of a new dispensation.

By hearkening to Heidegger and the other critics of modernity, one is hearkening to a new dispensation. One is becoming the change that one desires. One is living under the next dispensation today.

Thus perhaps one can excuse Heidegger for obscurity, for the medium is clearly part of the message. But if communicating this message was as important to Heidegger as it seems, you would think he would have striven for utmost clarity—that he would have tried to imitate Schopenhauer rather than to outdo Kant, Fichte, Hegel, and Schelling for Teutonic turbidness. He can't plead lack of talent, since his lecture courses are famously clear. He had to work hard to write texts as pretentious and maddeningly obscure as *Contributions to Philosophy*.

But there is nothing contradictory or self-defeating about a clear exposition of the nature and role of obscurity and hiddenness. Shadows, gaps, and abysses can have cleanly delineated edges. If Heidegger is right, then it really is of epochal importance that he find an able popularizer, his own Alan Watts.

Dugin's book, however, does not fit the bill. Dugin is attracted to all of Heidegger's worst rhetorical excesses, which he misinterprets in maximally metaphysical terms. For instance, Heidegger's notion of "fundamental ontology" refers to his quest for the meaning of Being (the meaning of meaning—the conditions that make worlds and dispensations of meaning possible). It has nothing to do with standard metaphysical notions of ultimate reality. According to Dugin, however:

> Starting out from the ontic (from *beings* in their most obvious, accessible characteristics), this time we must progress in another direction: we must not rise *above beings*, remaining bound to them and destroying them with this ambiguous relationship, as in the case of European metaphysics. Instead, we must glance *below*, delve into *beings' primordial source*—a place where nothing exists and where *Nothingness* is. But this *Nothingness* is not simply *non-beings* (generated from *beings*). This is Nothingness, which makes *beings* what they are, but which does not turn into *beings*. This *Nothingness* is life-giving, constituting all with its qui-

et power this is what *"fundamental-ontology"* is: the kind of ontology built along principally new patterns as compared to the entire preceding philosophy. *"Fundamental-ontology"* will let the new kind of *logos* shine. This time, however, it will not focus on *beings*, but on *Nothingness.* (pp. 63–64)

Heidegger's fundamental ontology is not, however, about the "primordial source" of beings. Again, it is about what makes it possible for beings to have meaning, to be taken up into worlds of intelligibility. This is characteristic of Dugin's exposition of Heidegger: It isn't any more readable than Heidegger, and half the time it isn't even Heidegger.

Dugin seems to understand Heidegger's *Ereignis* as a singular apocalyptic event that will inaugurate a new beginning, a new dispensation of meaning:

The *Seynsgeschichtliche* horizon of Heidegger's philosophy is oriented toward *Ereignis*. *Ereignis* is the culmination of *Being's* history, because at this point the whole process of *Seynsgeschichte* manifests itself in its true dimension: as *Being's* narration about itself in a reversed (inverted) form— the form of Being's oblivion (*Seinsvergessenheit*) and the triumph of nihilism. *Ereignis* is directly linked to the fact that at a certain point the entire cycle of Western European philosophy is being grasped in its true proportions and in terms of fundamental-ontological significance. And this process of grasping and comprehension forms the premise for *Seyn-Being's* advancement as it truly is—this time not through continuance in which it conceals itself, but rather through the single moment in which it reveals itself. (p. 148)

It is easy to get this sort of impression from Heidegger's posthumously publishing writings from the 1930s, such as *Contributions to Philosophy* or his 1948 essay "The Turn." But one should take the accounts of *Ereignis* that Heidegger published during his lifetime, particularly in his 1962 lecture "Time and Being," as his most considered view. And there Heidegger describes *Ereignis* as the generic structure of all dispensations of meaning: *All* ages of history emerge and take hold of us as inscrutable contingencies. Worlds of meaning happen like the rain: when we say, "It's raining," there is no "it" that is actually raining, just as there is no "it" that is sending a new dispensation. It just happens.

In the 1930s, Heidegger was full of apocalyptic hopes. His dalliance with National Socialism was in part motivated by his conviction that the German people had a leading role to play in ushering in a new dispensation. After the war, we hear nothing more about such philosophical geopolitics, which makes sense given the generally apolitical tenor of Heidegger's later thought. Dugin, however, seems to have adopted unaltered Heidegger's 1930s-style nationalism and hope for a political solution to the modern age. He has merely transposed them to Russia:

> Another beginning is a matter of the future, of those who will be upcoming, as Nietzsche dreamt. But the Sun does not rise in the West. And from now on, we have grasped the meaning of the sunset, necessary for moving toward the horizon *from another direction. Heidegger's another Beginning cannot address the people of the West. Therefore, it addresses us.* (p. 390)

When Dugin writes about liberalism, his ranting is often entertaining:

> Man of the global world, a Liberal, accepting and recognizing the normativity of the "American way of life," is the kind of person who is a patented idiot from the philosophical and etymological point of view, a documented idiot, an idiot parading his foolishness above his head like a banner. (pp. 163–64)

This, by the way, is the only passage in this admirable translation that one might be tempted to read in a Russian accent.

As a material object, this book is most impressive. The cover may look at bit like an English prog rock cover from the 1970s, but I like that sort of thing. The design and typesetting are quite elegant and readable, setting a new standard for Anglophone New Right publishing. I appreciate the use of footnotes rather than endnotes, and I particularly admire the care lavished on the extensive index. Radix has spared no labor or expense to bring out this volume.

This is definitely a prestige project: Heidegger is a prestigious thinker. A translation into English increases Dugin's prestige. Heidegger and Dugin bring prestige to Radix. Lest the Radix crew be suspected of anti-Semitism, Paul Gottfried helps out with a Preface and even says some good things about the book in the process.

But, in the end, my reservations about Dugin remain unchanged: He is opposed to a racial criterion of European identity; he is opposed to European ethnonationalism; he is an apologist for Russian multiculturalism and imperialism. I do not see how any of his works contribute to staving off the biological extinction of the white race. Heidegger can contribute to the metapolitical foundations for white salvation. But Dugin's Heidegger is not Heidegger, and Dugin himself is just a distraction.

Counter-Currents, November 21, 2014

NOTES ON HEIDEGGER & EVOLA

Evidence has recently emerged that Martin Heidegger read Julius Evola. In an article entitled "Ein spirituelles Umsturzprogramm" ("A Spiritual Revolution Program") published in the *Frankfurter allgemeine Zeitung*, December 30, 2015, Thomas Vasek reports on an important document he discovered:

> Julius Evola, the ultra-fascist Italian cultural philosopher, was eagerly read not only by Gottfried Benn, but also by Martin Heidegger as an unpublished note shows.
>
> The keyword of Martin Heidegger's note is "race"; below that appears, in the handwriting of the philosopher, the following sentence: "Wenn eine Rasse die Berührung mit dem, was allein Beständigkeit hat und geben kann— mit der Welt des Seyns—verloren hat, dann sinken die von ihr gebildeten kollektiven Organismen, welches immer ihre Größe und Macht sei, schicksalhaft in die Welt der Zufälligkeit herab." ["If a race has lost contact with what alone has and can give resistance—with the world of Beyng—then the collective organisms formed from it, whatever be their size and power, sink fatefully down into the world of contingency."] The quotation is taken verbatim from the book *Revolt Against the Modern World*, which was first published in German in 1935; only the spelling of "Being" has been Heideggerized.
>
> The author of the work was the Italian cultural philosopher and esotericist Julius Evola (1898–1974)—a racist and anti-Semite who revered the SS as an elite order, developed a Fascist racial doctrine, and a wrote a Preface to the *Protocols of the Elders of Zion*. After the war, the Italian fascists revered him. To this day he is considered a leading figure of the extreme Right across Europe. [. . .]
>
> The as yet unpublished excerpt could give new direction to the ongoing Heidegger controversy. Evola's name does not appear in Heidegger's published writings, and

Heidegger scholarship has taken little notice of him. Even the Italian philosopher Donatella di Cesare does not mention Evola in her book *Heidegger, the Jews, the Shoah* (2015). Yet textual comparisons suggest that Heidegger had not only read Evola, as this note indicates, but was also influenced by his ideas from the mid-thirties on, from his critique of science and technology, his anti-humanism and rejection of Christianity, to his "spiritual" racism. If this thesis is correct, then perhaps one could view the late Heidegger as a radical fascist esotericist who hoped that rule by a spiritual elite would bring about the reappearance of the gods.

Of course this single note establishes only that Heidegger read one of Evola's books, not that he read it "eagerly." Nor does it indicate what Heidegger thought of Evola. But it is still an important discovery. It could lead nowhere. (It could be Heidegger's sole reference to Evola.) Or it could be the tip of an iceberg. An Evola connection could end up throwing a great deal of light on Heidegger's interests and associations. No matter what the outcome, Vasek's discovery is the beginning of an important academic research project. Are there other references to Evola in the Heidegger papers? Did Heidegger read other works by Evola? Did he annotate Evola's books? Did Heidegger correspond with or meet Evola? (Both thinkers visited one another's homelands.)

I have long wondered if more mainstream thinkers of the Right like Heidegger and Carl Schmitt were aware of the Traditionalist school of Evola and René Guénon. This suspicion was based less on shared doctrines than on shared concerns. A philosopher's concerns are, in effect, the questions he is trying to answer; his doctrines are his attempts to answer them. Heidegger and Schmitt shared their Right-wing politics and critical eye on modernity with Evola and Guénon. That alone was sufficient reason to read them, even if they arrived at very different conclusions. Thus I was pleased to learn from Mircea Eliade's *Portugal Journal* that Schmitt said, "the most interesting man alive today is René Guénon" and that Eliade agreed, although his conviction sometimes wavered.[1] (Eliade also met Evola, corresponded with him, and read his works.) And now we have positive evidence that Heidegger read Evola.

I am skeptical, however, of Vasek's assertion that Heidegger was *influenced* by Evola from the mid-1930s on, specifically on such matters as science and technology, anti-humanism, the rejection of Christianity, and race and anti-Semitism. For one thing, Heidegger had rejected Christianity long before the 1930s. I eagerly anticipate Vasek's "textual comparisons," but my fear is that they will be superficial. For although both Heidegger and Evola shared a generally Right-wing political outlook and believed that technological modernity was the culmination of a long process of decline going back to antiquity, their ultimate philosophical premises were very different.

Evola's "world of Being" is essentially a Platonic realm of eternal, intelligible truth that stands in opposition to the "world of contingency," which is intelligible only insofar as it reflects the world of Being. By contrast, Heidegger's concept of "Beyng" (a rendering of his use of *Seyn*, the archaic spelling of the German *Sein*) refers to his concept of "*Ereignis*," which is actually an unintelligible contingency that establishes different reigning interpretations of man and world. Beyng is a source of historical meaning that can neither be understood nor controlled.

Evola believed that history's downward trajectory toward technological modernity and cultural decadence was a falling away from the world of Being into the world of contingency. Heidegger, however, regarded Evola's essentially Platonic outlook as part of the decline itself, indeed as standing very close to its beginning.

For Heidegger, the Platonic distillation of Being as pure intelligibility and intellect as the capacity to intuit the intelligible is false because it is an abstraction that overlooks a more fundamental unity, a mutual belonging of historical man and meaningful worlds. For Heidegger, we are too close to things and to ourselves, too involved in them, to fully understand or control

---

[1] Greg Johnson, "Mircea Eliade, Carl Schmitt, and René Guénon," *Counter-Currents*, July 15, 2013.

them. He believes that metaphysics posits both intelligible Being and a self-transparent intellect out of a drive for mastery. Thus the will to power that comes to fruition in global technological civilization is present at the very beginning of the metaphysical tradition.

Heidegger claims that we overlooked this fundamental unity because it, in effect, concealed itself. It is a historical event that cannot exist apart from man but nevertheless was not controlled by man either. The self-concealment of Beyng creates metaphysics. And metaphysics inaugurates the downward course of history, culminating in technological nihilism. Contra Evola, the beginning of decline is not a fall *from* metaphysics, but a fall *into* metaphysics.

In terms of the topic of Heidegger's unpublished note, namely race, Evola's objection to biological racism is that it is insufficiently metaphysical, overlooking "races of the soul" and "races of the spirit."[2] Heidegger, however, had a very different objection to biological race.

Throughout his philosophical career, Heidegger battled against false concepts of human nature. The common denominator of these false concepts is that they are universal. In the metaphysical tradition, the essence of man is what all men have in common. What reason tells us we all have in common is reason itself. Man is the rational animal.

The rational animal is not, however, a national animal. Because reason is one, humanity is one, so the human community should be one as well. Thus more particular attachments are illegitimate. If man is the rational animal, and reason grasps the universal, then reason is in effect a "view from nowhere" which can take us anywhere. The view from nowhere makes us citizens of everywhere. The rational animal is a citizen of the world; the *cosmos* is our *polis*; we have wings not roots.

Heidegger's word for human nature, however, is *Dasein*, which means "being here/there." *Dasein* is not a view from nowhere, but a view from somewhere. *Dasein*'s outlook on the

---

[2] Michael Bell, "Julius Evola's Concept of Race: A Racism of Three Degrees," *Counter-Currents*, February 6, 2011.

world is particular, not universal. It is particularized by space and time, and particularized by language and culture, which it shares with other *Dasein* in its community—but not with all of humanity. Heidegger is a philosopher of distinct identities, of the concrete, of the local, and of belonging, which is a mutual relationship: We belong to our world, and our world belongs to us. (The name of this concrete mutual belongingness is *Ereignis*.)

Heidegger's concept of *Dasein* is inherently political. We are not the rational animal but the national animal, and nation is defined by a common history, language, culture, and destiny. The politics of *Dasein* is, therefore, ethnonationalism.

Why not racial nationalism? Heidegger would not deny that race is part of ethnic identity. To be German one must be white. But there is more to being German than being white. Heidegger feared that defining identity in terms of biological race alone was another form of deracinating universalism. Not as universal and deracinating as "humanity," but with similar consequences. For if whiteness is essential, then it is easy to become indifferent to Germanness and Englishness, which is the road to deracination and homogenization. But for Heidegger this is a form of inauthenticity, a failure to own up to our full identity and carry forward the cultural and linguistic particularities of our heritage.

This is very different from Evola's metaphysical critique of biological racism. For Evola, biological race is too concrete and insufficiently metaphysical. For Heidegger, biological race is too abstract and metaphysical.

Nevertheless, despite the deep and fundamental rift between Heidegger's and Evola's views, Heidegger still chose to copy down Evola's words. That means *something*. The fact that Heidegger also changed "*Sein*" to "*Seyn*" was probably no slip of the pen. It means something too. Was Heidegger endorsing Evola's basic schema that the vitality of a people derives from its contact with a power that transcends its understanding and control? By changing *Sein* to *Seyn*, was he transposing Evola's metaphysical version of this theme into his own anti-metaphysical key? Translated into Heideggerian terms, Evola's schema is that a people, defined not in spiritual but cultural and historical terms, loses its vitality by turning away, not from Platonic ultimate reality, but from its participation in historically evolved practices of meaning—its traditions—and turning toward, not the world of contingency, but the modern mania for certainty and control, expressed in the racial sphere as eugenics and other public health measures. This is certainly consistent with Heidegger's discussions of race from the 1930s, including remarks from before the publication of the German translation of Evola's *Revolt Against the Modern World*.[3]

Some take the view that Heidegger's philosophy was essentially apolitical. Then he blundered into his unfortunate dalliance with National Socialism. Then he returned to an apolitical outlook. This is false. Heidegger's thought is ethnonationalist to the core. This implies that it never ceased being so. Thus the later Heidegger's politics simply went underground. It became hidden, occult, esoteric. Which means that Vasek may be on to something when he writes, "perhaps one could view the late Heidegger as a radical fascist esotericist who hoped that rule by a spiritual elite would bring about the reappearance of the gods."

My view is that Heidegger's disillusionment with National Socialism, which began in the middle of the 1930s, led him to search for a way of defining a post-totalitarian, ethnonationalist critique of globalizing, homogenizing modernity. In short, Heidegger was the first thinker of the New Right.

Counter-Currents, February 10, 2016

---

[3] See, for instance, Martin Heidegger, *Being and Truth* [1933–34], trans. Gregory Fried and Richard Polt (Bloomington: Indiana University Press, 2010), p. 138; *Mindfulness* [1939–1939], trans. Parvis Emad and Thomas Kalary (London: Bloomsbury, 2016), pp. 241–42; *Ponderings II–VI: Black Notebooks, 1931–1938*, trans. Richard Rojcewicz (Bloomington: Indiana University Press, 2016), p. 266; and especially *Ponderings XII–XV: Black Notebooks, 1939–1941*, trans. Richard Rojcewicz (Bloomington: Indiana University Press, 2016), p. 44.

GRADUATE SCHOOL WITH HEIDEGGER

The best decision I ever made was to pursue a Ph.D. in philosophy. I learned about the most important questions, I studied the most profound attempts to answer them, I acquired both the tools and the commitment to pursue the truth, and I became a better — that is, wiser — man in the process.

No, it did not lead to an academic career. Indeed, all my hopes, schemes, and efforts in that direction just left me discouraged, drained, and embittered. I had the knowledge, skills, and commitment. But I was the wrong race and the wrong sex; I definitely had the wrong politics; and, frankly, I think I took it too seriously and wanted it too much, which does not go over well with people who treat philosophy as merely a technical game or an adjunct to Leftist politics.

Hans-Georg Gadamer told a joke that perfectly sums up my view of academia. On the eighth day, God rose from his rest and decided that Creation needed one more thing to perfect it, so he created the German professor. But then the devil ruined it by creating the colleague.

It is just as well. Knowing what I know now, writing academic journal articles (which get read by maybe five or ten people) seems like fiddling while Rome burns.

Today, I am a teacher without colleagues, I can write whatever I please, my words are read by thousands, and instead of being confined to expensive books and obscure journals, my writings are available free to everyone.

Academia, moreover, has only gotten worse since I got my doctorate. Thus, unless you belong to a politically correct protected group that will guarantee you employment for what you *are* rather than what you *know*, I cannot recommend graduate school in philosophy, no matter how much you hunger for wisdom. And that goes for the rest of the humanities as well. The current reign of political correctness will make you miserable throughout your studies and unemployable once they are complete. And you won't learn that much anyway, because your professors will do more to close off the tradition than open it up to you. Moreover, there is very little chance you will find kindred spirits or even good company among your fellow graduate students.

Beyond that, graduate school is costly. Even with a full scholarship and stipend, it will be hard not to go into debt. And even if you don't leave graduate school with enormous debts, you will still have spent six to ten years getting a Ph.D. while other people your age are starting families and accruing assets. And any undergraduate loans you have will still be there.

Fortunately, it is no longer necessary to go to graduate school to get an excellent Ph.D.-level education in philosophy. For the price of a couple of shelves of books, you can attend the lectures of one of the greatest philosophers and most talented teachers of the twentieth century, namely Martin Heidegger. And instead of a troop of tattooed, perforated, sexually confused, and politically correct graduate students, your classmates will be such eminent twentieth-century thinkers as Hans-Georg Gadamer, Leo Strauss, Hannah Arendt, Karl Löwith, Hans Jonas, Herbert Marcuse, and Jean Beaufret.

The *Complete Edition* (*Gesamtausgabe*) of Heidegger's works contains fifty-two projected volumes of manuscripts, transcripts, and notes of Heidegger's lecture courses and seminars, spanning fifty-four years, from 1919 to 1973. By my count, these volumes contain materials from fifty-three lecture courses and more than forty seminars. A significant percentage of these volumes have already been translated into English, and it is probable that virtually all of them will be translated, given enough time.

Although the texts Heidegger prepared for publication are notoriously crabbed and obscure, his lecture courses are lucid and engaging. Heidegger was a legendary teacher, renowned both for the insightfulness and originality of what he said and the spell-bindingly charismatic way he said it. His most eminent students have recorded their impressions. Hans-Georg Gadamer writes:

It is impossible to exaggerate the drama of Heidegger's appearance in Marburg. Not that he was out for sensation. His appearance in the lecture hall certainly had something of a guaranteed effectiveness to it, but the unique thing about his person and his teaching lay in the fact that he identified himself fully with his work and radiated from that work. Because of him the lecture format became something totally new. It was no longer the "lesson presentation" of a professor who put his essential energy into research and publication.

The "great book" monologues lost their priority of place because of Heidegger. What he provided was the full investment of his energy, and what brilliant energy it was. It was the energy of a revolutionary thinker who himself visibly shrank from the boldness of his increasingly radical questions and who was so filled with the passion of his thinking that he conveyed to his listeners a fascination that was not to be broken. . . . Who among those who then followed him can forget the breathtaking swirl of questions that he developed in the introductory hours of the semester for the sake of entangling himself in the second or third of these questions and then, in the final hours of the semester, rolling up the deep-dark clouds of sentences from which the lightning flashed to leave us half stunned?[1]

Hannah Arendt had a similar experience:

. . . Heidegger's "fame" predates by about eight years the publication of *Sein und Zeit* (*Being and Time*) in 1927; indeed it is open to question whether the unusual success of this book—not just the immediate impact it had inside and outside the academic world but also its extraordinarily lasting influence, with which few of the century's publications can compare—would have been possible if it had not

---

[1] Hans-Georg Gadamer, *Philosophical Apprenticeships*, trans. Robert R. Sullivan (Cambridge: MIT Press, 1985), p. 48.

been preceded by the teacher's reputation among the students, in whose opinion, at any rate, the book's success merely confirmed what they had known for many years.

There was something strange about this early fame, stranger perhaps than the fame of Kafka in the early Twenties or of Braque and Picasso in the preceding decade, who were also unknown to what is commonly understood as the public and nevertheless exerted an extraordinary influence. For in Heidegger's case there was nothing tangible on which his fame could have been based, nothing written, save for notes taken at his lectures which circulated among students everywhere. These lectures dealt with texts that were generally familiar; they contained no doctrine that could have been learned, reproduced, and handed on. There was hardly more than a name, but the name traveled all over Germany like the rumor of the hidden king.[2]

Leo Strauss also found Heidegger immensely impressive:

One of the unknown young men in Husserl's entourage was Heidegger. I attended his lecture course from time to time without understanding a word, but sensed that he dealt with something of the utmost importance to man as man. I understood something on one occasion: when he interpreted the beginning of the *Metaphysics*. I had never heard nor seen such a thing—such a thorough and intensive interpretation of a philosophic text. On my way home I visited [Franz] Rosenzweig and said to him that compared to Heidegger, Max Weber, till then regarded by me as the incarnation of the spirit of science and scholarship, was an orphan child.[3]

---

[2] Hannah Arendt, "Martin Heidegger at Eighty," *New York Review of Books*, October 21, 1971.

[3] Leo Strauss, "A Giving of Accounts," *Jewish Philosophy and the Crisis of Modernity: Essays and Lectures in Modern Jewish Thought*, ed. Kenneth Hart Green (Albany: SUNY Press, 1997), p. 461.

What are the chances you will find such a teacher in any graduate program today? Fortunately, because of the publication of Heidegger's lectures and seminars, now you don't need to.

There are two ways to use Heidegger's lectures and seminars: some courses stand on their own, while others are commentaries on texts that should be read in conjunction. As you will discover, Heidegger's coverage of certain texts was sometimes highly selective. Sometimes he digressed from his outline or ran out of time. But these are no objections, because lesser teachers do the same things too. And if it didn't hurt Gadamer, Arendt, and Strauss, it probably won't hurt you.

As you will also discover, people strongly disagree with Heidegger's philosophy and his readings of other thinkers. But this is no objection either, because the same can be said of every lesser teacher as well.

One drawback of reading lecture courses is that you can't ask Heidegger questions. But trust me, if you were actually there, you probably would have been too intimidated to say anything anyway. Gadamer tells the story of one of Edmund Husserl's lectures, in which he spoke for an hour, took one question, spent another hour answering it, then dismissed the class. As Husserl left the lecture hall, he turned to Heidegger, who was his assistant at the time, and remarked on what an exciting discussion they'd had that day.[4] In truth, Heidegger was probably no better. And we should all be grateful, because you wouldn't want to be reading transcripts of graduate student questions anyway. (The most frustrating feature of the seminar notes is that the students' views—and confusions—often intrude.)

Another disadvantage of merely reading lecture courses is that one cannot discuss them with one's fellow students—although one can, of course, read what Gadamer, Arendt, Strauss, Löwith, and others had to say about Heidegger.

Both of these problems can be somewhat ameliorated by the internet. You can discuss Heidegger's lectures and seminars with people around the globe, including credentialed Heidegger

---

[4] *Philosophical Apprenticeships*, p. 36.

scholars, perhaps the very editors and translators of the volumes you are reading.

To that end, I have secured the domain name Heidegger.us. Although I do not have the time to run another website, I would be glad to work with responsible parties who are willing to create a web forum with sub-forums devoted to all of Heidegger's lecture courses and seminars. Although one cannot ask Heidegger questions, one might be able to get recognized Heidegger scholars to pinch-hit for him if the community becomes large and vibrant enough.

The rise of podcasting also provides a promising medium. It would be an interesting experiment for a talented speaker to perform and record audio versions of Heidegger's lectures.

Heidegger cannot provide a complete graduate education alone, although his expertise is far wider than most professors. But no graduate program consists merely of coursework. The core of a graduate curriculum is a comprehensive reading list, on which students are examined. I recommend that you adopt a reading list from a Ph.D. program that puts a strong emphasis on the history of philosophy.

One's coursework can never cover everything on such a reading list, so a significant portion of graduate study is self-education anyway. But, then again, one of the principal goals of graduate school is to produce educators—or, people who are at least *capable* of educating others, since you don't really know it unless you can pass it on—and your first student should always be yourself.

Most Ph.D. programs require eighteen to twenty lecture courses or seminars. Heidegger, however, left us more than ninety to choose from. Heidegger did not teach every subject, but most graduate students never take coursework from a whole philosophy faculty that is broader than what Heidegger offers alone. And if you really work through even half of Heidegger's lecture courses and seminars, you will be vastly better-educated than many newly-minted Ph.D.s.

But what if you are not ready for graduate-level study in philosophy? The answer is simple. Before you go to graduate school with Heidegger, I suggest you go to undergraduate school with

Kant, Hegel, and Nietzsche. One could get an excellent under-graduate-level education in philosophy by working through Kant's lectures on metaphysics, ethics, logic, and philosophical theology; Hegel's lectures on *The History of Philosophy*, *The Philosophy of World History*, *The Philosophy of Religion*, and *Aesthetics*; and Friedrich Nietzsche's lectures on early Greek philosophy (*The Pre-Platonic Philosophers* and *Philosophy in the Tragic Age of the Greeks*).[5] Like Heidegger, Kant and Hegel were terrible writers but engaging and accessible lecturers.

I also recommend supplementing one's graduate course-work with Alexandre Kojève's *Introduction to the Reading of Hegel: Lectures on the Phenomenology of Spirit* and Leo Strauss's lectures covering Aristophanes, Plato, Xenophon, Aristotle, Cicero, Machiavelli, Hobbes, Spinoza, Vico, Rousseau, Kant, Hegel, Marx, and the central questions of political philosophy.[6]

The Western intellectual tradition is too precious to be left in the hands of an ideologically corrupt and hostile educational system. This is particularly true of philosophy. Much of academia is simply a museum full of dead and taxidermied cultural curios. They are worthy products of human creativity, precious parts of our heritage that should be preserved rather than distorted and destroyed by ideologues and obscurantists. But they are of interest to few and of vital importance to none.

Philosophy, however, is of vital importance to everyone who

---

[5] All of these lecture courses are available in English translations.

[6] Only about half of Kojève's *Introduction à la Lecture de Hegel*, ed. Raymond Queneau (Paris: Gallimard, 1947) appears in *Introduction to the Reading of Hegel*, trans. James H. Nichols, Jr. (Ithaca: Cornell University Press, 1969). Audio recordings and transcripts of some of Strauss' lecture courses are available online at The Leo Strauss Center website, https://leostrausscenter.uchicago.edu/. Three of these lecture courses have now been published: Leo Strauss, *Leo Strauss on Nietzsche's* Thus Spoke Zarathustra, ed. Richard L. Velkley (Chicago: University of Chicago Press, 2017); *Leo Strauss on Political Philosophy: Responding to the Challenge of Positivism and Historicism*, ed. Catherine H. Zuckert (Chicago: University of Chicago Press, 2018); and *Leo Strauss on Hegel*, ed. Paul Franco (Chicago: University of Chicago Press, 2019).

wishes to lead a good life, for philosophy is the pursuit of wisdom, and wisdom is the ability to make right use of all things. Fortune deals some of us good hands, others bad ones. Wisdom is what allows us to play our cards well, so we lead the best lives possible. Thus everyone needs philosophy, which means that everyone needs philosophy teachers, which means that we need to find non-academic paths to mastering philosophy and passing it on.

Graduate school with Heidegger — combining a good comprehensive reading list, Heidegger's lectures and seminars, and internet-based discussion — is merely one possible alternative to academia as usual. I urge you to try it, or to propose something better.

There are few if any teachers alive today who can offer you a better graduate education than Heidegger. And thanks to the publication of his lecture courses and seminars, the "hidden king" of thought can now reign openly, as long as there are students who wish to hear him.

APPENDIX:
Heidegger's Lecture Courses & Seminars

The following list comprises Heidegger's lecture courses and seminars. It does not include Heidegger's published and unpublished books and essays, stand-alone lectures, notebooks, and correspondence, although these of course can supplement his lectures and seminars. Some entries are repeated, since they fall under multiple headings. The initial numbers refer to the volumes of Heidegger's *Complete Edition*. The years in parentheses refer to the original year(s) of the lecture course or seminar.

Introductions to Philosophy
27: *Einleitung in die Philosophie* (1928).
    Translation in preparation as *Introduction to Philosophy*.

Ancient Philosophy Surveys
22: *Grundbegriffe der antiken Philosophie* (1926).
    Translated as *Basic Concepts of Ancient Philosophy*
83: *Seminare: Platon – Aristoteles – Augustinus*

Early Greek Philosophy

35: *Der Anfang der abendländischen Philosophie (Anaximander und Parmenides)* (1932).

Translated as *The Beginning of Western Philosophy: Interpretation of Anaximander and Parmenides*

54: *Parmenides* (1942).

Translated as *Parmenides.*

55: *Heraklit.*

1. *Der Anfang des abendländischen Denkens (Heraklit)* (1943).
2. *Logik. Heraklits Lehre vom Logos* (1944).

Translated as *Heraclitus: The Inception of Occidental Thinking* and *Logic: Heraclitus's Doctrine of the Logos.*

8: *Was heisst Denken?* (1951–52), Part II.

Translated as *What Is Called Thinking?*

15: *Heraklit* with Eugen Fink (1966-67).

Translated as *Heraclitus Seminar.*

Plato

19: *Platon: Sophistes* (1924).

Translated as *Plato's Sophist.*

34: *Vom Wesen der Wahrheit. Zu Platons Höhlengleichnis und Theätet* (1931).

Translated as *The Essence of Truth.* This title is not the "On the Essence of Truth" in *Pathmarks* and *Basic Writings.*

36/37: *Sein und Wahrheit.*

1. *Die Grundfrage der Philosophie* (1933).
2. *Vom Wesen der Wahrheit* (1933–34).

Translated as *Being and Truth.*

Aristotle

61: *Phänomenologische Interpretationen zu Aristoteles: Einführung in die phänomenologische Forschung* (1921).

Translated as *Phenomenological Interpretations of Aristotle.*

62: *Phänomenologische Interpretationen ausgewählter Abhandlungen des Aristoteles zur Ontologie und Logik* (1922).

18: *Grundbegriffe der aristotelischen Philosophie* (1924).

Translated as *Basic Concepts of Aristotelian Philosophy.*

33: *Aristoteles: Metaphysik IX* (1931).

Translated as *Aristotle's Metaphysics Theta 1–3: On the Essence and Actuality of Force.*

Survey: Medieval to Kant
23: *Geschichte der Philosophie von Thomas v. Aquin bis Kant* (1926).

Leibniz
26: *Metaphysische Anfangsgründe der Logik im Ausgang von Leibniz* (1928).
Translated as *The Metaphysical Foundations of Logic.*
10: *Der Satz vom Grund* (1955–56).
Translated as *The Principle of Reason.*

Leibniz & Kant
84: *Seminare: Leibniz – Kant*

Kant
25: *Phänomenologische Interpretation von Kants Kritik der reinen Vernunft* (1927).
Translated as *Phenomenological Interpretation of Kant's Critique of Pure Reason.*
31: *Vom Wesen der menschlichen Freiheit. Einleitung in die Philosophie* (1930).
Translated as *The Essence of Human Freedom.*
41: *Die Frage nach dem Ding. Zu Kants Lehre von den transzendentalen Grundsätzen* (1935).
Translated as *What Is a Thing?*

German Idealism Surveys
28: *Der Deutsche Idealismus (Fichte, Hegel, Schelling) und die philosophische Problemlage der Gegenwart* (1929).
Translation in preparation as *German Idealism.*
86: *Seminare: Hegel – Schelling*

Herder
85: *Vom Wesen der Sprache: Die Metaphysik der Sprache und die Wesung des Wortes; zu Herders Abhandlung »Über den Ursprung der Sprache«* (1939).

Translated as *On the Essence of Language.*

Hegel
32: *Hegels Phänomenologie des Geistes* (1930).
Translated as *Hegel's Phenomenology of Spirit.*

Hölderlin
39: *Hölderlins Hymnen »Germanien« und »Der Rhein«* (1934).
Translated as *Hölderlin's Hymns "Germania" and "The Rhein."*
52: *Hölderlins Hymne »Andenken«* (1941).
Translated as *Hölderlin's Hymn "Remembrance."*
53: *Hölderlins Hymne »Der Ister«* (1942).
Translated as *Hölderlin's Hymn "The Ister."*

Schelling
42: *Schelling: Über das Wesen der menschlichen*; a.k.a. *Schelling: Vom Wesen der menschlichen Freiheit (1809)* (1936).
Translated as *Schelling's Treatise on the Essence of Human Freedom.*
49: *Die Metaphysik des deutschen Idealismus. Zur erneuten auslegung von Schelling: Philosophische untersuchungen über das Wesen der menschlichen Freiheit und die damit zusammen-hängenden Gegenstände (1809)* (1941).

Nietzsche
43: *Nietzsche: Der Wille zur Macht als Kunst* (1936).
Translated as *The Will to Power as Art.*
44: *Nietzsches Metaphysische Grundstellung im abendländischen Denken: Die ewige Wiederkehr des Gleichen* (1937).
Translated as *The Eternal Recurrence of the Same.*
46: *Nietzsches II. Unzeitgemässe Betrachtung* (1938).
Translated as *Interpretation of Nietzsche's Second Untimely Meditation*
47: *Nietzsches Lehre vom Willen zur Macht als Erkenntnis* (1939).
Translated as *The Will to Power as Knowledge.*
48: *Nietzsche: Der europäische Nihilismus* (1940).
Translated as *European Nihilism.*
50: *Nietzsches Metaphysik* (1941–42).

Einleitung in die Philosopie – Denken und Dichten (1944–45).
Nietzsches Metaphysik was translated as "Nietzsche's Metaphysics"
Einleitung in die Philosopie was translated as *Introduction to Philosophy – Thinking and Poetizing.*
87: *Seminare: Nietzsche. Übungen SS 1937. Nietzsches metaphysische Grundstellung. Sein und Schein* (1937)
8: *Was heisst Denken?* (1951–52), Part I.
Translated as *What Is Called Thinking?*

Jünger
90: *Zu Ernst Jünger*

Phenomenology
56/57: *Zur Bestimmung der Philosophie.*
  1: *Die Idee der Philosophie und das Weltanschauungsproblem* (1919).
  2: *Phänomenologie und transzendentale Wertphilosophie* (1919).
  3: Appendix: *Über das Wesen der Universität und des akademischen Studiums* (1919).
  Translated as *Towards the Definition of Philosophy.*
58: *Grundprobleme der Phänomenologie* (1919).
  Translated as *The Basic Problems of Phenomenology.*
59: *Phänomenologie der Anschauung und des Ausdrucks. Theorie der philosophischen Begriffsbildung* (1920).
  Translated as *Phenomenology of Intuition and Expression.*
63: *Ontologie: Hermeneutik der Faktizität* (1923).
  Translated as *Ontology: The Hermeneutics of Facticity.*
17: *Einführung in die phänomenologische Forschung*; a.k.a. *Der Beginn der neuzeitlichen Philosophie* (1923).
  Translated as *Introduction to Phenomenological Research.*
20: *Prolegomena zur Geschichte des Zeitbegriffs* (1925).
  Translated as *History of the Concept of Time.*

Phenomenology of Religion
60: *Phänomenologie des religiösen Lebens.*
  1. *Einleitung in die Phänomenologie der Religion* (1920–21).
  2. *Augustinus und der Neuplatonismus* (1922).

3. *Die philosophischen Grundlagen der mittelalterlichen Mystik* (Outlines and sketches of an undelivered lecture course, 1918–19).

Translated as *The Phenomenology of Religious Life.*

Metaphysics

24: *Die Grundprobleme der Phänomenologie* (1927).

Translated as *The Basic Problems of Phenomenology.*

29/30: *Die Grundbegriffe der Metaphysik: Welt, Endlichkeit, Einsamkeit* (1929).

Translated as *The Fundamental Concepts of Metaphysics.*

36/37: *Sein und Wahrheit.*

1. *Die Grundfrage der Philosophie* (1933).

2. *Vom Wesen der Wahrheit* (1933–34).

Translated as *Being and Truth.*

40: *Einführung in die Metaphysik* (1935).

Translated as *Introduction to Metaphysics.*

51: *Grundbegriffe* (1941).

Translated as *Basic Concepts.*

88: *Einübung in das Denken.*

1. *Die metaphysischen Grundstellungen des abendländischen Denkens.*

2. *Die Bedrohung der Wissenschaft.*

Logic

21: *Logik: Die frage nach der Wahrheit* (1925).

Translated as *Logic: The Question of Truth.*

38: *Logik als die Frage nach dem Wesen der Sprache* (1934).

Translated as *Logic as the Question Concerning the Essence of Language.*

45: *Grundfragen der Philosophie. Ausgewählte »Probleme« der »Logik«* (1937).

Translated as *Basic Questions of Philosophy.*

Counter-Currents, February 3, 2016

RECOMMENDED READING

EIGHT ESSENTIAL BOOKS BY HEIDEGGER

Heidegger was an amazingly productive philosopher. His *Complete Edition* runs to more than 100 volumes, and there will be many more volumes of correspondence. We can, however, arrive at a list of essential volumes by looking at the works that Heidegger published in his own lifetime. Heidegger's posthumous works are, of course, important for documenting the development of his ideas and deepening our understanding of his published works. But, nevertheless, Heidegger had ample time and motive to publish all of his essential ideas during his lifetime, so that is where we should look first.

Heidegger is a notoriously difficult stylist. But he was a brilliant lecturer, and his lecture courses are far more accessible than the works he prepared directly for publication. Thus I have included four volumes of lecture courses in this list.

My first three recommendations are Heidegger's *magum opus*, *Being and Time* (1927), and two lecture courses that provide essential context.

1. *History of the Concept of Time: Prolegomena,* translated by Theodore Kisiel (Bloomington: Indiana University Press, 1985).
2. *Being and Time,* translated by John Macquarrie and Edward Robinson (New York: Harper & Row, 1962).
3. *The Basic Problems of Phenomenology,* translated by Albert Hofstadter (Bloomington: Indiana University Press, 1982).

Eventually, every reader of Heidegger will have to conquer *Being and Time*, which made Heidegger's reputation and is the most influential work of twentieth-century philosophy. But despite its wealth of exciting and suggestive ideas, actually reading *Being and Time* is a terrible slog.

A useful preparation for reading *Being and Time* is the 1925 lecture course *History of the Concept of Time: Prolegomena,* which is extremely helpful in situating the project of *Being and Time* in terms of Edmund Husserl's phenomenology and also covers with greater clarity many topics that Heidegger treats in *Being and Time* in his crabbed and ponderous academic style. *History of the Concept of Time* is the only volume in this list that was published after Heidegger's death in 1976, but before he died, he had put it on the fast track to publication, and it appeared in 1979. It is one of Heidegger's most exciting works.

There are two English translations of *Being and Time:* John Macquarrie and Edward Robinson (1962) and Joan Stambaugh and Dennis Schmitt (2010). (Avoid Stambaugh's solo translation from 1996.) Neither is perfect, but I got much more out of Macquarrie and Robinson's translation. It is stylistically thornier than Stambaugh and Schmitt, but for some reason it made a stronger impression.

Being and Time itself was never finished, but one can get a sense of how the book would have been completed by reading another highly lucid 1927 lecture course, *The Basic Problems of Phenomenology,* which deals with the question of Being in Kant, Aristotle, Medieval Scholasticism, and Descartes. *The Basic Problems of Phenomenology* was the first volume of Heidegger's *Complete Edition.* It was published in 1975, the year before he died.

The next three volumes collect Heidegger's major essays and lectures after *Being and Time.*

4. *Basic Writings,* edited by David F. Krell (New York: Harper & Row, 2008).
5. *Off the Beaten Track,* edited and translated by Julian Young and Kenneth Haynes (Cambridge: Cambridge University Press, 2002).
6. *Poetry, Language, Thought,* edited and translated by Albert Hofstadter (New York: Harper & Row, 1971).

These essays vary in difficulty from moderate to extreme, but all of them are richly rewarding. I recommend fourteen essays in particular.

Heidegger's *Basic Writings* are not basic in the sense of elementary or simple, but basic in the sense of foundational. The following eight essays are essential.

- ❖ "What Is Metaphysics?"
- ❖ "On the Essence of Truth"
- ❖ "The Origin of the Work of Art"
- ❖ "Letter on Humanism"
- ❖ "The Question Concerning Technology"
- ❖ "Building, Dwelling, Thinking"
- ❖ "The Way to Language"
- ❖ "The End of Philosophy and the Task of Thinking."

Note that "The Origin of the Work of Art" is abridged in the 1977 first edition of *Basic Writings* but is complete in the subsequent (1993 and 2008) editions.

Another anthology, *The Heidegger Reader*, edited by Günther Figal, translated by Jerome Veith (Bloomington: Indiana University Press, 2009), is an interestingly conceived and useful work, but it cannot rival *Basic Writings*, simply because *Basic Writings* includes genuinely basic writings that *The Heidegger Reader* excludes.

Off the Beaten Track contains six long essays, including another (somewhat improved) translation of "The Origin of the Work of Art," which I have already recommended in *Basic Writings*. Of the five essays that remain, the most essential are:

- ❖ "The Age of the World Picture"
- ❖ "Nietzsche's Word 'God is Dead'"
- ❖ "Anaximander's Saying"

"The Age of the World Picture" deals with modernity. It is one of Heidegger's clearest and most exciting essays, and it should be read before "The Question Concerning Technology."

"Nietzsche's Word" is the fruit of Heidegger's intensive study of Nietzsche in the 1930s and 1940s.

"Anaximander's Saying" tells us more about Heidegger than Anaximander, but that's fine. It contains some of

Heidegger's most precise formulations of his concepts of Being, truth, and the history of Being; if it weren't so long, I would recommend that you read it first.

Heidegger's essays on language and poetry are some of his richest. In *Poetry, Language, Thought,* the essential essays are:

- ❖ "The Thing"
- ❖ "Language"
- ❖ ". . . Poetically Man Dwells . . ."

Finally, there are these essential lecture courses:

7. *Introduction to Metaphysics,* translated by Gregory Fried and Richard Polt (New Haven: Yale University Press, 2000).
8. *What Is Called Thinking?,* translated by J. Glenn Gray (New York: Harper & Row, 1968).

Introduction to Metaphysics is a lecture course given in 1935 and published in 1953. (Avoid the earlier translation by Ralph Mannheim). I imagine many casual browsers have purchased *Introduction to Metaphysics* thinking it is for beginners, only to have their minds blown—in a bad way. If you know what you are getting into, it will blow your mind in a good way. For me, this book best captures Heidegger's reputation for classroom wizardry. For a commentary on *Introduction to Metaphysics,* see Collin Cleary's essay "Heidegger: An Introduction for Anti-Modernists" in his *What Is a Rune? & Other Essays,* ed. Greg Johnson (San Francisco: Counter-Currents, 2015).

What Is Called Thinking? (1954) collects Heidegger's last two lecture courses, from 1951 and 1952. The first course deals with Nietzsche, the second with early Greek philosophy, but both also serve as overviews of Heidegger's late thought, which had attained its full maturity. Written with great clarity, it is something of a swan song. Hannah Arendt's blurb for J. Glenn Gray's excellent translation is no exaggeration: "For an acquaintance with the thought of Heidegger, *What Is Called Thinking?* is as important as *Being and Time.* It is the only systematic presentation of the thinker's late philosophy and . . . it is perhaps the most exciting of his books."

Reading these books and essays is equivalent to an upper-level undergraduate survey of Heidegger plus a graduate-level seminar on *Being and Time*.

MORE ADVANCED READING IN HEIDEGGER

If you work your way through the eight volumes above, you will be able to explore the rest of Heidegger's works on your own, based on your particular interests. But don't miss the following volumes. This list is evenly divided between works Heidegger published during his lifetime and his posthumous lectures and notebooks.

1. *Towards the Definition of Philosophy*, translated by Ted Sadler (London: Continuum, 2000).
2. *The Phenomenology of Religious Life*, translated by Matthias Fritsche and Jennifer Anna Gosetti-Ferencei (Bloomington: Indiana University Press, 2004).
3. *The Fundamental Concepts of Metaphysics: World, Finitude, Solitude*, translated by William McNeill and Nicholas Walker (Bloomington: Indiana University Press, 1995).
4. *Nietzsche*, 4 vols., edited by David Farrell Krell, translated by David Farrell Krell, Frank A. Capuzzi, and Joan Stambaugh (New York: Harper & Row, 1979, 1982, 1984, 1987).
5. *The End of Philosophy*, translated by Joan Stambaugh (New York: Harper & Row, 1973).
6. *Pathmarks*, edited by William McNeill (Cambridge: Cambridge University Press, 1998).
7. *The Bremen and Freiburg Lectures: Insight into that Which Is and Basic Principles of Thinking*, translated by Andrew J. Mitchell (Bloomington: Indiana University Press, 2012).
8. *On the Way to Language*, translated by Peter D. Herz with Joan Stambaugh (New York: Harper & Row, 1971).

9. *On Time and Being*, translated by Joan Stambaugh (New York: Harper & Row, 1972).
10. *Ponderings II–VI: Black Notebooks 1931–1938*, translated by Richard Rojcewicz (Bloomington: Indiana University Press, 2016).

The list begins with three of Heidegger's most fascinating volumes of lectures.

Towards the Definition of Philosophy collects two early lecture courses from 1919. They reveal a surprising unity and maturity to Heidegger's thought, even in his earliest lectures. For instance, he already uses "*Ereignis*" as a technical term.

The Phenomenology of Religious Life contains two lecture courses, plus notes for a third undelivered course, dating from 1918–1921, in which we see Heidegger's ideas of *Dasein*, facticity, formal indication, and the temporality of human existence emerging from a dialogue with Christian thinkers like Saint Paul and Saint Augustine.

The Fundamental Concepts of Metaphysics from 1929–30, like *Being and Time*, is a magnificent torso of an unfinished work. The best part is the phenomenology of boredom, which is at least in part autobiographical. After publishing *Being and Time*, Heidegger seemed to suffer a sort of post-partum depression and to be at a loss as to how to continue its outline by shifting from a transcendental to a historical approach to meaning. It is tempting to regard his plunge into politics, which took place around the same time, as a kind of respite from this impasse.

The original German edition of *Nietzsche* was published in two volumes in 1961. It collects four lecture courses on Nietzsche from the late 1930s and early 1940s, plus supplemental lectures and essays. Originally published in English in four volumes, the *Nietzsche* lectures are now available in two large paperbacks: *Nietzsche*: vols. 1 and 2 and *Nietzsche*: vols. 3 and 4. Three of the supplementary essays from the original German edition have been published in *The End of Philosophy*.

In addition to dealing with metaphysics and Nietzsche, these courses also document Heidegger's increasing distance from National Socialism. The Nietzsche lectures are quite readable. The essays are tough going. But, all told, the *Nietzsche* volumes are a magnificent intellectual achievement and must be read by everyone who takes Heidegger or Nietzsche seriously.

Pathmarks, The Bremen and Freiburg Lectures, On the Way to Language, and *On Time and Being* collect some of Heidegger's most important essays and lectures from the 1930s to the 1960s. The Bremen Lectures are the basis for Heidegger's classic essays "The Question Concerning Technology," "The Thing," and "The Turn." *On the Way to Language* is particularly important for understanding how our participation in evolved linguistic and cultural practices is the horizon in which we encounter the world. It really deserves a new translation. There is some overlap between these volumes and collections like *Basic Writings* and *Poetry, Language, Thought*, but that is unavoidable.

I am not a fan of Heidegger's unpublished treatises like *Contributions to Philosophy, Mindfulness, The Event*, and *The History of Beyng*. They strike me as belabored, repetitive, needlessly obscure, and often merely provisional. Moreover, they don't throw that much light on Heidegger's published works.

But I do recommend the so-called *Black Notebooks*, the ongoing series of essays, aphorisms, and reflections that will occupy the last nine volumes of the *Complete Edition*. The *Black Notebooks* contain many ideas that Heidegger never published in any form, including his reflections on the Third Reich, World War II, and post-war Germany. In style, they are usually accessible, often candid and unpretentious, and sometimes quite angry and acerbic. The first three volumes of *Black Notebooks* have been translated into English by Richard Rojcewicz. I have listed the first above. If you read it, you will want to read more.

Indiana University Press published its last volume in the set in 2017. I hope the project has not been abandoned. All nine volumes should eventually be translated.

Six Essential Books About Heidegger

There is an immense secondary literature on Heidegger, but most of it is no more accessible than Heidegger himself. These books are significant exceptions.

1. Graham Harman, *Heidegger Explained: From Phenomenon to Thing* (Chicago: Open Court, 2007).
2. Rüdiger Safranski, *Martin Heidegger: Between Good and Evil*, translated by Ewald Osers (Cambridge: Harvard University Press, 1999).
3. Thomas Sheehan, *Making Sense of Heidegger: A Paradigm Shift* (New York: Rowman & Littlefield, 2014).
4. Graeme Nicholson, *Illustrations of Being: Drawing Upon Heidegger and Upon Metaphysics* (Atlantic Highlands, N.J.: Humanities Press, 1992).
5. Michael Zimmerman, *Heidegger's Confrontation with Modernity: Technology, Politics, and Art* (Bloomington: Indiana University Press, 1990).
6. Richard Polt, *Time and Trauma: Thinking Through Heidegger in the Thirties* (New York: Rowman & Littlefield, 2019)

Graham Harman's *Heidegger Explained* is the best introductory book on Heidegger. It is short (around 180 pages), clearly and engagingly written, chronologically organized, explains all of Heidegger's most important technical terms, identifies his basic thought patterns, gives a tour of his most important books, and never loses sight of the essential.

Harman is correct about Heidegger's conception of Being as the presence and absence of that which is present and absent (beings), but he does not deal with Heidegger's distinction between ontology (which deals with Being) and fundamental ontology (which deals with the meaning, truth, clearing, or event of Being, i.e., how Being is given to us). (See chapters 4 and 5 in this volume.)

The best biography of Heidegger is Rüdiger Safranski's *Martin Heidegger: Between Good and Evil*.

Thomas Sheehan's *Making Sense of Heidegger* is one of the most important books ever written on Heidegger because it deals squarely with the essential distinction for understanding Heidegger: between Being and the meaning or "sense" of Being. This distinction is overlooked by most Heidegger scholars. Sheehan's book is discussed extensively above in chapter 5.

Graeme Nicholson's *Illustrations of Being* is one of the best books on Heidegger and the metaphysical tradition. Nicholson correctly understands Being (the presence/absence of beings) and the meaning of Being (the presence/absence of Being itself). Contra deconstructionists who would simply dispense with metaphysics altogether, Nicholson stresses that on Heideggerian terms, the metaphysical tradition contains truths of permanent validity.

Michael Zimmerman's *Heidegger's Confrontation with Modernity: Technology, Politics, and Art* is one of the best books ever published about Heidegger. It is clearly written and thrilling to read. It deals with Heidegger's critique of modernity in the context of the Conservative Revolution, extensively discusses his relationship to Ernst Jünger, deals with Heidegger's relationship with National Socialism, and situates it all in the context of the development of his fundamental ontology.

Richard Polt's *Time and Trauma* is the most up-to-date account of Heidegger's political engagement and philosophical ideas during the Third Reich. I discuss it extensively in chapter 10 above.

SIX SPECIALIZED BOOKS ON HEIDEGGER

If you *really* get into Heidegger, here are some more advanced pieces of scholarship that I have found helpful.

1. John van Buren, *The Young Heidegger: Rumor of the Hidden King* (Bloomington: Indiana University Press, 1994).
2. Theodore Kisiel, *The Genesis of Heidegger's Being and Time* (Berkeley: University of California Press, 1993).
3. Jeffrey Malpas, *Heidegger's Topology: Being, Place, World* (Cambridge: MIT Press, 2008).
4. Charles Bambach, *Heidegger's Roots: Nietzsche, National Socialism, and the Greeks* (Ithaca: Cornell University Press, 2003).
5. Robert Mugerauer, *Heidegger and Homecoming: The Leitmotif in the Later Writings* (Toronto: University of Toronto Press, 2008).
6. Bret W. Davis, *Heidegger and the Will: On the Way to Ge-*

lassenheit (Evanston: Northwestern University Press, 2007).

The volumes by van Buren and Kisiel are detailed studies of the development of Heidegger's thought up through *Being and Time*. The volumes by Malpas, Bambach, and Mugerauer deal with the central importance of place and roots in Heidegger's thought, which is essential to his critique of philosophical and political universalism and his advocacy of ethnic nationalism. Bret Davis examines the development of Heidegger's critique of the will, which is essential to understanding his critiques of modernity and totalitarianism.

TWO IMPORTANT PIECES OF BACKGROUND READING

The ideal preparation for reading Heidegger is to spend at least five years intensely studying Aristotle and Husserl. But who has time for that? The next best thing is to find some good secondary literature.

Thomas Sheehan's *Making Sense of Heidegger* includes an excellent discussion of Heidegger's debts to Aristotle, as does Kisiel's *The Genesis of Heidegger's Being and Time*.

As for Husserl, I highly recommend two books by Robert Sokolowski:

1. Robert Sokolowski, *Husserlian Meditations: How Words Present Things* (Evanston: Northwestern University Press, 1974).
2. Robert Sokolowski, *Presence and Absence: A Philosophical Study of Language and Being* (Bloomington: Indiana University Press, 1978).

Husserlian Meditations is about Husserl, whereas *Presence and Absence* is a Husserlian study of language and being. Like Heidegger, Sokolowski does Husserlian phenomenology without the language of transcendental subjectivity. Sokolowski gives the clearest introduction I know to the deep thought patterns of Husserlian and Heideggerian phenomenology. Once you know Heidegger's basic moves, you always have a sense of where he is taking you. Otherwise baffling texts suddenly become intelligible. (Graham Harman's *Heidegger Explained* performs a similar function by emphasizing the importance of Heidegger's recurring twofold, threefold, and fourfold schemas.)

Three additional works that help situate Heidegger in terms of the transcendental tradition of Kant and Husserl are:

1. Steven Galt Crowell, *Husserl, Heidegger, and the Space of Meaning: Paths Toward Transcendental Phenomenology* (Evanston: Northwestern University Press, 2001).
2. Chad Engelland, *Heidegger's Shadow: Kant, Husserl, and the Transcendental Turn* (New York: Routledge, 2017).
3. Steven Crowell and Jeff Malpas, eds. *Transcendental Heidegger* (Stanford: Stanford University Press, 2007).

FIVE FUN BOOKS ON HEIDEGGER

You'll learn something from these books, but I recommend them simply because they are fun.

1. Heinrich Wiegand Petzet, *Encounters and Dialogues with Martin Heidegger, 1929–1976*, translated by Parvis Emad and Kenneth Maly (Chicago: University of Chicago Press, 1993).
2. Hans-Georg Gadamer, *Philosophical Apprenticeships*, translated by Robert R. Sullivan (Cambridge: MIT Press, 1987).
3. Digne Meller Marcovicz, *Martin Heidegger: Photos, 23. September 1966, 16. u. 17. Juni 1968* (Frankfurt: Vittorio Klostermann, 1985).
4. Adam Sharr, *Heidegger's Hut* (Cambridge: MIT Press, 2006).
5. Jef Costello, *Heidegger in Chicago: A Comedy of Errors* (San Francisco: Counter-Currents, 2015).

Heinrich Wiegand Petzet's memoir *Encounters and Dialogues with Martin Heidegger, 1929–1976* gives a vivid sense of the highly cultivated people in Heidegger's generally Right-wing and National Socialist milieu.

Hans-Georg Gadamer, Heidegger's most distinguished student, relates many endearing anecdotes about Heidegger in his memoir *Philosophical Apprenticeships*.

Digne Meller Marcovicz's photos of Heidegger, both at his home in Freiburg and his vacation cottage, the "hut," are quite charming, in a Tolkienesque sort of way.

Adam Sharr's *Heidegger's Hut* is about Heidegger's cabin in the Black Forest. If someone writes an entire book about your vacation cottage, that's a pretty clear indication that you have a cult following.

Jef Costello's *Heidegger in Chicago: A Comedy of Errors* is an absurdist novel about what might have happened if Heidegger had visited the United States and bumped into the Duchess of Windsor, Michael Jackson, Charles Manson, Yukio Mishima, Savitri Devi, and others. Naturally, he would have been misunderstood.

INDEX

Numbers in bold refer to a whole chapter or section devoted to a particular topic.

ABOUT THE AUTHOR

GREG JOHNSON, Ph.D. is Editor-in-Chief of Counter-Currents Publishing Ltd. and the *Counter-Currents* webzine (http://www.counter-currents.com/).

He is the author of *Confessions of a Reluctant Hater* (San Francisco: Counter-Currents, 2010; expanded edition, 2016), *Trevor Lynch's White Nationalist Guide to the Movies* (Counter-Currents, 2012), *New Right vs. Old Right* (Counter-Currents, 2013), *Son of Trevor Lynch's White Nationalist Guide to the Movies* (Counter-Currents, 2015), *Truth, Justice, & a Nice White Country* (Counter-Currents, 2015), *In Defense of Prejudice* (Counter-Currents, 2017), *You Asked for It: Selected Interviews*, vol. 1 (Counter-Currents, 2017), *The White Nationalist Manifesto* (Counter-Currents, 2018), *Toward a New Nationalism* (Counter-Currents, 2019), *Return of the Son of Trevor Lynch's CENSORED Guide to the Movies* (Counter-Currents, 2019), *From Plato to Postmodernism* (Counter-Currents, 2019), and *It's Okay to Be White* (Ministry of Truth, 2020).

He is editor of *North American New Right*, vol. 1 (Counter-Currents, 2012); *North American New Right*, vol. 2 (Counter-Currents, 2017); *The Alternative Right* (Counter-Currents, 2018); *Dark Right: Batman Viewed from the Right* (with Gregory Hood, Counter-Currents, 2018); Julius Evola, *East and West: Comparative Studies in Pursuit of Tradition* (with Collin Cleary, Counter-Currents, 2018); Collin Cleary, *Summoning the Gods: Essays on Paganism in a God-Forsaken World* (Counter-Currents, 2011); Collin Cleary, *What is a Rune? & Other Essays* (Counter-Currents, 2015); Jonathan Bowden, *Western Civilization Bites Back* (Counter-Currents, 2014); Jonathan Bowden, *Extremists: Studies in Metapolitics* (Counter-Currents, 2017), and many other books.

His writings have been translated into Czech, Danish, Dutch, Estonian, French, German, Greek, Hungarian, Norwegian, Polish, Portuguese, Russian, Slovak, Spanish, Swedish, and Ukrainian.

Ingram Content Group UK Ltd.
Milton Keynes UK
UKHW041344110423
419977UK00003B/62